SEE THE LORD'S SALVATION: A LENTEN STUDY OF EXODUS

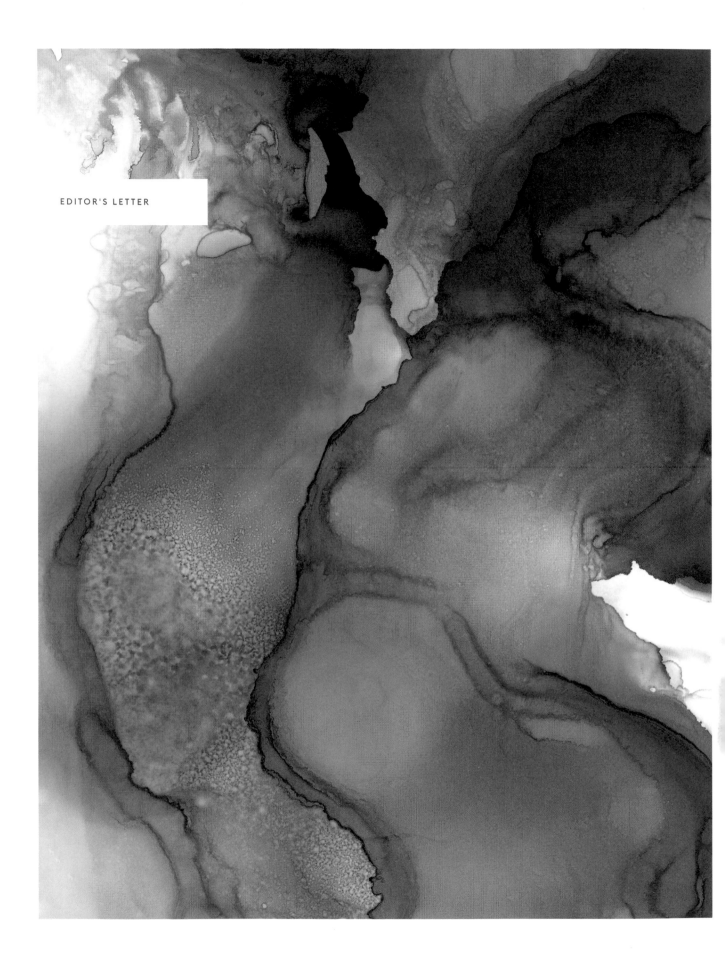

THIS BOOK BELONGS TO

_____

START DATE

_____

EDITORIAL

EDITORS-IN-CHIEF
Raechel Myers & Amanda Bible Williams

CONTENT DIRECTOR
Russ Ramsey, MDiv., ThM.

MANAGING EDITOR
Jessica Lamb

EDITOR
Kara Gause

CREATIVE

CREATIVE DIRECTOR
Ryan Myers

ART DIRECTOR
Amanda Barnhart

DESIGNER
Kelsea Allen

PRODUCTION DESIGNER
Julie Allen

ARTWORK
Ashley Mahlberg
@inkreel

RECIPES
Angela Cay Hall
@seedplantwatergrow

ILLUSTRATIONS
Maya Ish-Shalom
@maya_ishshalom

@SHEREADSTRUTH

SHEREADSTRUTH.COM

SUBSCRIPTION INQUIRIES
orders@shereadstruth.com

SHE READS TRUTH™

This book was printed offset in Nashville, Tennessee, on 70# Lynx Opaque Text. Cover is 100# Cougar Opaque with a soft touch lamination.

One Saturday last fall I listened to the entire book of Exodus.

I'd never read the book in one sitting before, and I wanted to get a sense of Exodus as a piece of literature, rather than a series of chapters and verses. By the end I was moved to tears.

There were plenty of interruptions, so it took the entire day, but there was a sweetness in our home as the story of God's salvation filled the air from breakfast to dinner. For a while, my young daughter lay at my feet and fiddled with toys, listening to the story. As the Israelites crossed the Red Sea and Miriam sang her song, my girl sang a version she'd learned in school, "Sing to the LORD, for he is highly exalted; he has thrown the horse and its rider into the sea!" (Ex 15:21).

In the afternoon, we listened as God gave instructions to build the tabernacle. I noticed my husband find a place on the nearby sofa to listen as God appointed and equipped Bezalel to be the chief designer and executor of the process. I could tell by his interest that these chapters hold a special place in my husband's design-loving heart.

As evening set in, I moved to our back porch to listen to the final few chapters. God gathered my family to listen with me as "the glory of the LORD filled the tabernacle" (40:35). I replayed the last few paragraphs several times, in tearful awe of the nearness of God to His people then, and His nearness to us still. God seemed more holy and magnificent than ever before. But in reality, He's the same—yesterday, today, forever (Heb 13:8).

"

The book of Exodus is a story of salvation.

The book of Exodus is a story of salvation. As the Israelites escaped Egypt, Pharaoh and his army in hot pursuit, Moses said to the people, "Don't be afraid. Stand firm and see the LORD's salvation that he will accomplish for you today" (14:13). God saved His people that day and He saves us still, through the completed work of Christ.

We've divided this Lenten study of Exodus into three sections. The first, "The Road Out," covers the story of the exodus of God's people. The second, "For Glory and Beauty," details the building of the tabernacle and its contents. And the third, "See the Lord's Salvation," invites us to read in real time the events of Holy Week, from Palm Sunday to Resurrection Sunday.

As always, we've included lots of great extras in this book. You'll find delicious recipes, a map of the exodus, a timeline of Moses' life, illustrations of the tabernacle and priestly garments, Easter hymns, and even a macramé activity that might help you slow down a bit this Lenten season.

The narratives in this book are not just stories. They are our heritage—our story of salvation. We look forward to reading them with you.

Raechel

Raechel Myers
EDITOR-IN-CHIEF

Introduction

Days 1-2

The Road Out

Days 3-14: Exodus 1-17

For Glory and Beauty

Days 15-41: Exodus 18-40

2

See the Lord's Salvation

Days 42-49: Holy Week

3

Recipes

Almond Squares with Toasted Coconut Glaze

122

Strawberry and Chia Parfait

68

Morning Skillet

166

Bella and Broth Noodle Bowl

142

Black Pepper Salmon and Zucchini Noodle Bowl

96

Activity

Diamond Macramé Wall Hanging

36

Extras   +

She Reads Truth is a community of women dedicated to reading the Word of God every day. The Bible is living and active, breathed out by God, and we confidently hold it higher than anything we can do or say. This book focuses primarily on Scripture, with bonus resources to facilitate deeper engagement with God's Word.

SCRIPTURE READING

This Lent book includes the entire text of Exodus divided into daily readings, with supplemental scriptures to help you understand the meaning and biblical context of the passage. The last week focuses on the events of Holy Week.

JOURNALING SPACE

Each weekday features space for personal reflection and prayer.

GRACE DAY

Use Saturdays to pray, rest, and reflect on what you've read.

For added community and conversation, join us in the **Lent 2018: See the Lord's Salvation** reading plan, which begins February 12, on the She Reads Truth app and SheReadsTruth.com.

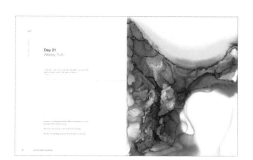

WEEKLY TRUTH

Sundays are set aside for weekly Scripture memorization.

Design on Purpose

The She Reads Truth creative team is driven by our confidence in two truths found in Scripture.

We are created to create. We learn this in the early chapters of Genesis as God the Creator makes man in His own image. Some of us are instilled with a drive to craft ideas, solve problems, write songs, paint murals, construct spaces, draw, sketch, or design. Some creatively build businesses, homes, meals, and stories. But everyone creates.

God values beauty and quality. Thirteen chapters of Exodus record the details of God's artistic design for His holy tabernacle and its contents. That's forty percent of this book! God even appointed a creative director, Bezalel, and filled him with His "Spirit, with wisdom, understanding, and ability in every craft" to design and build the tabernacle to His specifications (31:3). The text uses a form of the word "skillful" 27 times, and repeatedly emphasizes that certain elements of the tabernacle are created for the specific purpose of adding beauty.

In light of these truths, our creative team eagerly embraced the challenge of designing a She Reads Truth study book for this book of the Bible that celebrates the high calling of good design.

The artwork in this book is by Ashley Mahlberg. Her specialized technique of using alcohol ink and gessobord to create unpredictable marbled art pieces resonates with the narrative of Exodus. As the ink travels on the gessobord, the colors blend and collide to create both soft and hard moments in the piece—moments

> **"** The book of Exodus celebrates the high calling of good design.

that reflect the complexity of the Exodus story. The tender care with which Moses is placed in a basket as a baby is juxtaposed with the Israelites' treacherous journey out of captivity. The vast wilderness of the desert stands starkly against the abundance of God's provision, with bread raining from the sky and water flowing from a rock. Ashley's art, both aesthetically and symbolically, became our foundation for the rest of the design choices.

We chose bold cerulean and plum as the main colors for this book. Cerulean creates a sense of refreshment and grounding, while plum traditionally reminds us of God's power and beauty. These colors are used throughout to grab your attention, signify a section change, or highlight a verse.

Helvetica, often used for subway or transportation signage, seemed to be the perfect fit for this book since even the word "exodus" implies travel. Helvetica offers clear guidance with clean letter shapes, while managing to not draw attention to itself.

In order to maintain a cohesive project, we asked food blogger Angela Hall to share her moody and darkly beautiful food photography for Grace Day recipes. And since Exodus gives us so much detail about the tabernacle and priestly garments, we had New York-based designer Maya Ish-Shalom create helpful illustrations so you can envision the designs God gives Moses. (A fun fact about Maya: she was born in Israel and studied at Bezalel Academy of Arts and Design in Jerusalem.)

There's an old Shaker design philosophy that says, "Don't make something unless it is both necessary and useful; but if it is both necessary and useful, don't hesitate to make it beautiful." God's Word doesn't need good design to be necessary or useful, but it is deserving of it. We hope this study reminds you that the Lord's salvation, presented here in His Word, is all three.

For glory and beauty,

THE SHE READS TRUTH CREATIVE TEAM

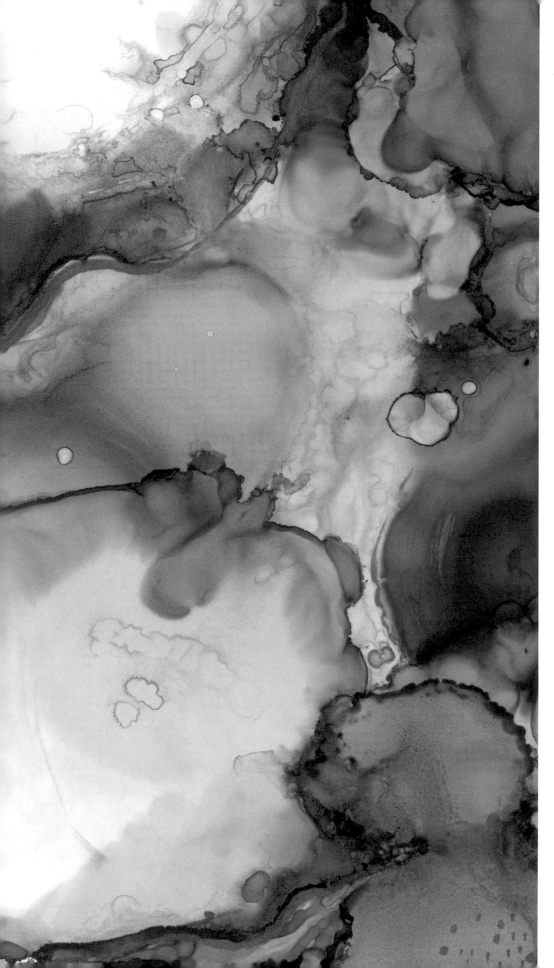

Featured Artists

Paintings

ASHLEY MAHLBERG

Ashley is an abstract artist who focuses on creating original artwork inspired by the colors and natural beauty of the Pacific Northwest. She lives in Burlington, Washington, with her husband and son.

Illustration

MAYA ISH-SHALOM

Maya is a Brooklyn-based illustrator originally from Tel Aviv, Israel, where she graduated from Bezalel Academy of Arts and Design in Jerusalem. Her bright and textured style displays itself in bold patterns and compositions.

Recipes

ANGELA CAY HALL

Angela is a visual storyteller and photographer. She uses food grown locally to her Nashville, Tennessee, home as inspiration for her recipes.

She Reads
Exodus

On the Timeline:

Along with the other four books of the Pentateuch, Exodus has long been considered the work of Moses. Moses could have written Exodus at any time during a 40-year span after the Israelites finished constructing and dedicating the tabernacle at Mount Sinai (1445 BC) and before his death in the land of Moab (about 1406 BC). The events in Exodus pick up where Genesis ends, with the death of Joseph around 1805 BC, and conclude with the building of the tabernacle in 1445 BC.

A Little Background:

True to its name, Exodus is centered around the departure of God's people from Egypt, where they were held as slaves to Pharaoh. The date of the exodus itself is disputed, but biblical evidence favors 1446 BC. First Kings 6:1 tells us the exodus occurred 480 years before Solomon's fourth year as king, which was likely 966 BC. In Judges 11:26, Jephthah said Israel had been living in regions of Palestine for 300 years. Jephthah lived around 1100 BC, which dates the end of the wilderness journey around 1400 BC.

Message and Purpose:

The book of Exodus shows God at work for the people of Israel, so that He "might dwell among them" (29:46). God rescued the Israelites in order to make Himself known, not only by the exercise of His power but also through an ongoing covenant relationship based on His patience, grace, and forgiveness. The record of what the Lord did for the Israelites provided grounds for them to recognize Him as their God who deserved their complete loyalty and obedience, and made clear to them their identity as God's people.

Give Thanks for the Book of Exodus:

Exodus is the high point of redemptive history in the Old Testament. Many patterns and concepts from Exodus are revisited elsewhere in Scripture, especially in the past, present, and future work of Jesus. From deliverance and provision, to God's glory and presence, the themes of Exodus find their fulfillment in Christ.

The Heart of Lent

AMANDA BIBLE WILLIAMS

From the moment our first parents were deceived by the serpent, we have been striving. "You will eat bread by the sweat of your brow until you return to the ground," God told them (Gn 3:19). And so we toil—whether sitting at a desk or plowing the land, studying for classes or scouring job listings, growing children or crops or companies. The work is not easy and, truth be told, it overtakes us. It is no surprise, then, that this is how we view the work of our salvation: as a matter of toiling and striving.

If achievement and acclaim are our chief end, effort is our primary means. That is the world's gospel, but it is not the gospel of Jesus. The salvation offered by God in Jesus Christ does not follow the world's rule of merit. All of Scripture is a story of God's unearned love and unmerited faithfulness toward a rebellious people. It is an exodus story, where the primary job of the recuee is to trust the Rescuer.

Isaiah 30:15 reads: "For the Lord GOD, the Holy One of Israel, has said: 'You will be delivered by returning and resting; your strength will lie in quiet confidence.'" It's a deep breath, this verse. A deliverance that comes from rest and quiet? What a dream.

But rest and quiet—much less returning to our holy God—do not come naturally to our Genesis 3 hearts. Our tendency is to run. The verse continues: "But you are not willing. You say, 'No! We will escape on horses'—

therefore you will escape!—and, 'We will ride on fast horses'—but those who pursue you will be faster" (Is 30:15-16).

We cannot outrun, outwit, or outwork our sin. No amount of effort or grit or good intention can deliver us from the world of death and dust. As hopeless as it may sound, this truth rings of freedom! **We cannot deliver ourselves, but the One who can deliver us has come.**

Lent is a long, slow season where we pause to remember who we are, who God is, and what Jesus has done. We are made from dust with love and intention, in the image of our Creator (Gn 1:27). We have sinned and we are sinners, incapable of saving ourselves (Rm 6:23). Jesus Christ is the perfect expression of God's eternal love and faithfulness, given to reconcile us to Himself (Col 1:19-20). We are invited to repent of our sin, return to our merciful and compassionate God, and rest in the freedom of His grace and forgiveness (Ac 3:19-20).

His love for us cannot be outdone or undone. Enter this season of repentance and remembrance with humility, willing to see and confess your sin. And enter with confidence, trusting in the completed work of Jesus Christ on your behalf. Don't bother running away on fast horses or hiding behind your best efforts. Run to Him, and rest. ◖

February 12, 2018

Day 1

GENESIS 3:17-19, PSALM 78:1-7, ISAIAH 30:15-18,
JOEL 2:12, ACTS 3:19-20, ROMANS 3:22-23,
COLOSSIANS 2:6-14

Genesis 3:17-19

¹⁷ And he said to the man, "Because you listened to your wife and ate from the tree about which I commanded you, 'Do not eat from it':

The ground is cursed because of you.
You will eat from it by means of painful labor
all the days of your life.
¹⁸ It will produce thorns and thistles for you,
and you will eat the plants of the field.
¹⁹ You will eat bread by the sweat of your brow
until you return to the ground,
since you were taken from it.
For you are dust,
and you will return to dust."

Psalm 78:1-7

Lessons from Israel's Past

A Maskil of Asaph.

¹ My people, hear my instruction;
listen to the words from my mouth.
² I will declare wise sayings;
I will speak mysteries from the past—
³ things we have heard and known
and that our fathers have passed down to us.
⁴ We will not hide them from their children,
but will tell a future generation
the praiseworthy acts of the LORD,

his might, and the wondrous works
he has performed.
⁵ He established a testimony in Jacob
and set up a law in Israel,
which he commanded our fathers
to teach to their children
⁶ so that a future generation—
children yet to be born—might know.
They were to rise and tell their children
⁷ so that they might put their confidence in God
and not forget God's works,
but keep his commands.

Isaiah 30:15-18

¹⁵ For the Lord GOD, the Holy One of Israel, has said:
"You will be delivered by returning and resting;
your strength will lie in quiet confidence.
But you are not willing."
¹⁶ You say, "No!
We will escape on horses"—
therefore you will escape!—
and, "We will ride on fast horses"—
but those who pursue you will be faster.
¹⁷ One thousand will flee at the threat of one,
at the threat of five you will flee,
until you remain
like a solitary pole on a mountaintop
or a banner on a hill.

The Lord's Mercy to Israel

[18] Therefore the Lord is waiting to show you mercy,
and is rising up to show you compassion,
for the Lord is a just God.
All who wait patiently for him are happy.

Joel 2:12
God's Call for Repentance

Even now—
    this is the Lord's declaration—
turn to me with all your heart,
with fasting, weeping, and mourning.

Acts 3:19-20

[19] Therefore repent and turn back, so that your sins may be wiped out, [20] that seasons of refreshing may come from the presence of the Lord, and that he may send Jesus, who has been appointed for you as the Messiah.

Romans 3:22-23

[22] The righteousness of God is through faith in Jesus Christ to all who believe, since there is no distinction. [23] For all have sinned and fall short of the glory of God.

Colossians 2:6-14

[6] So then, just as you have received Christ Jesus as Lord, continue to live in him, [7] being rooted and built up in him and established in the faith, just as you were taught, and overflowing with gratitude.

[8] Be careful that no one takes you captive through philosophy and empty deceit based on human tradition, based on the elements of the world, rather than Christ. [9] For the entire fullness of God's nature dwells bodily in Christ, [10] and you have been filled by him, who is the head over every ruler and authority. [11] You were also circumcised in him with a circumcision not done with hands, by putting off the body of flesh, in the circumcision of Christ, [12] when you were buried with him in baptism, in which you were also raised with him through faith in the working of God, who raised him from the dead. [13] And when you were dead in trespasses and in the uncircumcision of your flesh, he made you alive with him and forgave us all our trespasses. [14] He erased the certificate of debt, with its obligations, that was against us and opposed to us, and has taken it away by nailing it to the cross.

Month   Day

Understanding Exodus Through the Cross

RUSS RAMSEY

Jesus said the book of Exodus was about Him.

To the religious leaders who wanted to kill Him, Jesus said, "if you believed Moses, you would believe me, because he wrote about me" (Jn 5:46). And when He appeared to the travelers on the road to Emmaus after He had risen, "beginning with Moses and all the Prophets, he interpreted for them the things concerning himself in all the Scriptures" (Lk 24:27). Passages like these tell us there is no better way to read to the book of Exodus than in light of Jesus' cross and empty tomb.

The entire story of Exodus rests on promises God made to His people. There is the promise the Lord made to Abraham four hundred years earlier—to take his descendants as His own and love them with an everlasting love (Gn 12:1-3). Exodus says it was because of this ancient promise to Abraham that God delivered the people of Moses (Ex 2:24). This has always been the way of the Lord. The grace He extends to you and me is not based on how He feels about us in any given moment. His faithfulness is anchored in ancient promises He made long before we were born. God doesn't change. His steadfast love endures forever (Ps 136:1).

But there is an even greater promise at work in Exodus than the one He made to Abraham. When Adam and Eve sinned against the Lord, God swore that one would come who would crush evil's head (Gn 3:15). The life, death, and resurrection of Jesus are the fulfillment of that promise. Every word of Scripture that follows rests on God's vow to redeem and restore His sinful, wayward people to Himself, which He accomplished through the ministry of His Son.

Exodus points to how Jesus would save us. We see Him in the Passover lamb, in the bread from heaven, in the water that flowed when the rock was struck, and in the burning bush which spoke the name "I AM." We see Him in the liberation of a people oppressed by tyranny and enslaved to a kingdom of this world. Even more, we see Jesus as the presence of God coming down from heaven to dwell among His people (Ex 40:34-35; Jn 1:14).

When we stop to ask why any of these events took place, the answer is because God made a promise. He made a promise to rescue us from slavery to sin (Rom 6:18). He made a promise to lead us through the wilderness of this life (Ps 23). And He made a promise to bring us into our eternal promised home (2Co 5:1). All these things have been accomplished for us through the sacrifice of our perfect Passover Lamb, Jesus—the Son of God (1Pt 1:18-19).

The Bible is a book of promises made and promises kept, and Jesus is at the center of them all (2Co 1:20). ◼

February 13, 2018

Day 2

GENESIS 15:13-15, PSALM 136, LUKE 24:13-32

Genesis 15:13-15

¹³ Then the LORD said to Abram, "Know this for certain: Your offspring will be resident aliens for four hundred years in a land that does not belong to them and will be enslaved and oppressed. ¹⁴ However, I will judge the nation they serve, and afterward they will go out with many possessions. ¹⁵ But you will go to your fathers in peace and be buried at a good old age."

Psalm 136
God's Love Is Eternal

¹ Give thanks to the LORD, for he is good.
   His faithful love endures forever.
² Give thanks to the God of gods.
   His faithful love endures forever.
³ Give thanks to the Lord of lords.
   His faithful love endures forever.
⁴ He alone does great wonders.
   His faithful love endures forever.
⁵ He made the heavens skillfully.
   His faithful love endures forever.
⁶ He spread the land on the waters.
   His faithful love endures forever.
⁷ He made the great lights:
   His faithful love endures forever.
⁸ the sun to rule by day,
   His faithful love endures forever.
⁹ the moon and stars to rule by night.
   His faithful love endures forever.

¹⁰ He struck the firstborn of the Egyptians
   His faithful love endures forever.
¹¹ and brought Israel out from among them
   His faithful love endures forever.
¹² with a strong hand and outstretched arm.
   His faithful love endures forever.
¹³ He divided the Red Sea
   His faithful love endures forever.
¹⁴ and led Israel through,
   His faithful love endures forever.
¹⁵ but hurled Pharaoh and his army into the Red Sea.
   His faithful love endures forever.
¹⁶ He led his people in the wilderness.
   His faithful love endures forever.
¹⁷ He struck down great kings
   His faithful love endures forever.
¹⁸ and slaughtered famous kings—
   His faithful love endures forever.
¹⁹ Sihon king of the Amorites
   His faithful love endures forever.
²⁰ and Og king of Bashan—
   His faithful love endures forever.
²¹ and gave their land as an inheritance,
   His faithful love endures forever.
²² an inheritance to Israel his servant.
   His faithful love endures forever.
²³ He remembered us in our humiliation
   His faithful love endures forever.

²⁴ and rescued us from our foes.

His faithful love endures forever.

²⁵ He gives food to every creature.

His faithful love endures forever.

²⁶ Give thanks to the God of heaven!

His faithful love endures forever.

Luke 24:13-32
The Emmaus Disciples

¹³ Now that same day two of them were on their way to a village called Emmaus, which was about seven miles from Jerusalem. ¹⁴ Together they were discussing everything that had taken place. ¹⁵ And while they were discussing and arguing, Jesus himself came near and began to walk along with them. ¹⁶ But they were prevented from recognizing him. ¹⁷ Then he asked them, "What is this dispute that you're having with each other as you are walking?" And they stopped walking and looked discouraged.

¹⁸ The one named Cleopas answered him, "Are you the only visitor in Jerusalem who doesn't know the things that happened there in these days?"

¹⁹ "What things?" he asked them.

So they said to him, "The things concerning Jesus of Nazareth, who was a prophet powerful in action and speech before God and all the people, ²⁰ and how our chief priests and leaders handed him over to be sentenced to death, and they crucified him. ²¹ But we were hoping that he was the one who was about to redeem Israel. Besides all this, it's the third day since these things happened. ²² Moreover, some women from our group astounded us. They arrived early at the tomb, ²³ and when they didn't find his body, they came and reported that they had seen a vision of angels who said he was alive. ²⁴ Some of those who were with us went to the tomb and found it just as the women had said, but they didn't see him."

²⁵ He said to them, "How foolish and slow you are to believe all that the prophets have spoken! ²⁶ Wasn't it necessary for the Messiah to suffer these things and enter into his glory?" ²⁷ Then beginning with Moses and all the Prophets, he interpreted for them the things concerning himself in all the Scriptures.

²⁸ They came near the village where they were going, and he gave the impression that he was going farther. ²⁹ But they urged him, "Stay with us, because it's almost evening, and now the day is almost over." So he went in to stay with them.

³⁰ It was as he reclined at the table with them that he took the bread, blessed and broke it, and gave it to them. ³¹ Then their eyes were opened, and they recognized him, but he disappeared from their sight. ³² They said to each other, "Weren't our hearts burning within us while he was talking with us on the road and explaining the Scriptures to us?"

Month   Day

Notes

Section 1
The Road Out

Exodus 1-17

The Greek word *exodus* means "the road out."
These first chapters of the book of Exodus tell the
story of Israel's road out of slavery in Egypt into
a place of total dependence upon the God who
leads them.

Day 3
Israel Oppressed in Egypt

Exodus 1
Israel Oppressed in Egypt

These are the names of the sons of Israel who came to Egypt with Jacob; each came with his family:

2 Reuben, Simeon, Levi, and Judah;
3 Issachar, Zebulun, and Benjamin;
4 Dan and Naphtali; Gad and Asher.

5 The total number of Jacob's descendants was seventy; Joseph was already in Egypt.

6 Joseph and all his brothers and all that generation eventually died. 7 But the Israelites were fruitful, increased rapidly, multiplied, and became extremely numerous so that the land was filled with them.

8 A new king, who did not know about Joseph, came to power in Egypt. 9 He said to his people, "Look, the Israelite people are more numerous and powerful than we are. 10 Come, let's deal shrewdly with them; otherwise they will multiply further, and when war breaks out, they will join our enemies, fight against us, and leave the country." 11 So the Egyptians assigned taskmasters over the Israelites to oppress them with forced labor. They built Pithom and Rameses as supply cities for Pharaoh. 12 But the more they oppressed them, the more they multiplied and spread so that the Egyptians came to dread the Israelites. 13 They worked the Israelites ruthlessly 14 and made their lives bitter with difficult labor in brick and mortar and in all kinds of fieldwork. They ruthlessly imposed all this work on them.

[15] The king of Egypt said to the Hebrew midwives—the first whose name was Shiphrah and the second whose name was Puah— [16] "When you help the Hebrew women give birth, observe them as they deliver. If the child is a son, kill him, but if it's a daughter, she may live." [17] The midwives, however, feared God and did not do as the king of Egypt had told them; they let the boys live. [18] So the king of Egypt summoned the midwives and asked them, "Why have you done this and let the boys live?"

[19] The midwives said to Pharaoh, "The Hebrew women are not like the Egyptian women, for they are vigorous and give birth before the midwife can get to them."

[20] So God was good to the midwives, and the people multiplied and became very numerous. [21] Since the midwives feared God, he gave them families. [22] Pharaoh then commanded all his people: "You must throw every son born to the Hebrews into the Nile, but let every daughter live."

Exodus 2
Moses's Birth and Adoption

[1] Now a man from the family of Levi married a Levite woman. [2] The woman became pregnant and gave birth to a son; when she saw that he was beautiful, she hid him for three months. [3] But when she could no longer hide him, she got a papyrus basket for him and coated it with asphalt and pitch. She placed the child in it and set it among the reeds by the bank of the Nile. [4] Then his sister stood at a distance in order to see what would happen to him.

[5] Pharaoh's daughter went down to bathe at the Nile while her servant girls walked along the riverbank. She saw the basket among the reeds, sent her slave girl, took it, [6] opened it, and saw him, the child—and there he was, a little boy, crying. She felt sorry for him and said, "This is one of the Hebrew boys."

[7] Then his sister said to Pharaoh's daughter, "Should I go and call a Hebrew woman who is nursing to nurse the boy for you?"

[8] "Go," Pharaoh's daughter told her. So the girl went and called the boy's mother. [9] Then Pharaoh's daughter said to her, "Take this child and nurse him for me, and I will pay your wages." So the woman took the boy and nursed him. [10] When the child grew older, she brought him to Pharaoh's daughter, and he became her son. She named him Moses, "Because," she said, "I drew him out of the water."

Moses in Midian

[11] Years later, after Moses had grown up, he went out to his own people and observed their forced labor. He saw an Egyptian striking a Hebrew, one of his people. [12] Looking all around and seeing no one, he struck the Egyptian dead and

And God heard their groaning; and God remembered his covenant...

EXODUS 2:24

hid him in the sand. [13] The next day he went out and saw two Hebrews fighting. He asked the one in the wrong, "Why are you attacking your neighbor?"

[14] "Who made you a commander and judge over us?" the man replied. "Are you planning to kill me as you killed the Egyptian?"

Then Moses became afraid and thought, "What I did is certainly known."

[15] When Pharaoh heard about this, he tried to kill Moses. But Moses fled from Pharaoh and went to live in the land of Midian, and sat down by a well.

[16] Now the priest of Midian had seven daughters. They came to draw water and filled the troughs to water their father's flock. [17] Then some shepherds arrived and drove them away, but Moses came to their rescue and watered their flock. [18] When they returned to their father Reuel, he asked, "Why have you come back so quickly today?"

[19] They answered, "An Egyptian rescued us from the shepherds. He even drew water for us and watered the flock."

[20] "So where is he?" he asked his daughters. "Why then did you leave the man behind? Invite him to eat dinner."

[21] Moses agreed to stay with the man, and he gave his daughter Zipporah to Moses in marriage. [22] She gave birth to a son whom he named Gershom, for he said, "I have been a resident alien in a foreign land."

[23] After a long time, the king of Egypt died. The Israelites groaned because of their difficult labor; and they cried out; and their cry for help because of the difficult labor ascended to God. [24] And God heard their groaning; and God remembered his covenant with Abraham, with Isaac, and with Jacob; [25] and God saw the Israelites; and God knew.

Genesis 35:11-12

[11] God also said to him,

"I am God Almighty.

Be fruitful and multiply. A nation, indeed an assembly of nations, will come from you, and kings will descend from you. [12] I will give to you the land that I gave to Abraham and Isaac. And I will give the land to your future descendants."

Matthew 2:13-23
The Flight into Egypt

¹³ After they were gone, an angel of the Lord appeared to Joseph in a dream, saying, "Get up! Take the child and his mother, flee to Egypt, and stay there until I tell you. For Herod is about to search for the child to kill him." ¹⁴ So he got up, took the child and his mother during the night, and escaped to Egypt. ¹⁵ He stayed there until Herod's death, so that what was spoken by the Lord through the prophet might be fulfilled: Out of Egypt I called my Son.

The Massacre of the Innocents

¹⁶ Then Herod, when he realized that he had been outwitted by the wise men, flew into a rage. He gave orders to massacre all the boys in and around Bethlehem who were two years old and under, in keeping with the time he had learned from the wise men. ¹⁷ Then what was spoken through Jeremiah the prophet was fulfilled:

¹⁸ A voice was heard in Ramah,
weeping, and great mourning,
Rachel weeping for her children;
and she refused to be consoled,
because they are no more.

The Return to Nazareth

¹⁹ After Herod died, an angel of the Lord appeared in a dream to Joseph in Egypt, ²⁰ saying, "Get up, take the child and his mother, and go to the land of Israel, because those who intended to kill the child are dead." ²¹ So he got up, took the child and his mother, and entered the land of Israel. ²² But when he heard that Archelaus was ruling over Judea in place of his father Herod, he was afraid to go there. And being warned in a dream, he withdrew to the region of Galilee. ²³ Then he went and settled in a town called Nazareth to fulfill what was spoken through the prophets, that he would be called a Nazarene.

Day 4
The Lord Calls Moses

Exodus 3
Moses and the Burning Bush

Meanwhile, Moses was shepherding the flock of his father-in-law Jethro, the priest of Midian. He led the flock to the far side of the wilderness and came to Horeb, the mountain of God. ² Then the angel of the LORD appeared to him in a flame of fire within a bush. As Moses looked, he saw that the bush was on fire but was not consumed. ³ So Moses thought, "I must go over and look at this remarkable sight. Why isn't the bush burning up?"

⁴ When the LORD saw that he had gone over to look, God called out to him from the bush, "Moses, Moses!"

"Here I am," he answered.

⁵ "Do not come closer," he said. "Remove the sandals from your feet, for the place where you are standing is holy ground." ⁶ Then he continued, "I am the God of your father, the God of Abraham, the God of Isaac, and the God of Jacob." Moses hid his face because he was afraid to look at God.

⁷ Then the LORD said, "I have observed the misery of my people in Egypt, and have heard them crying out because of their oppressors. I know about their sufferings, ⁸ and I have come down to rescue them from the power of the Egyptians and to bring them from that land to a good and spacious land, a land flowing with milk and honey—the territory of the Canaanites, Hethites, Amorites, Perizzites, Hivites, and Jebusites. ⁹ So because the Israelites' cry for help has come to me, and I have also seen the way the Egyptians are oppressing them, ¹⁰ therefore, go. I am sending you to Pharaoh so that you may lead my people, the Israelites, out of Egypt."

---

¹¹ But Moses asked God, "Who am I that I should go to Pharaoh and that I should bring the Israelites out of Egypt?"

¹² He answered, "I will certainly be with you, and this will be the sign to you that I am the one who sent you: when you bring the people out of Egypt, you will all worship God at this mountain."

¹³ Then Moses asked God, "If I go to the Israelites and say to them, 'The God of your fathers has sent me to you,' and they ask me, 'What is his name?' what should I tell them?"

¹⁴ God replied to Moses, "I AM WHO I AM. This is what you are to say to the Israelites: I AM has sent me to you." ¹⁵ God also said to Moses, "Say this to the Israelites: The LORD the God of your fathers, the God of Abraham, the God of Isaac, and the God of Jacob, has sent me to you. This is my name forever; this is how I am to be remembered in every generation.

¹⁶ "Go and assemble the elders of Israel and say to them: The LORD, the God of your fathers, the God of Abraham, Isaac, and Jacob, has appeared to me and said: I have paid close attention to you and to what has been done to you in Egypt. ¹⁷ And I have promised you that I will bring you up from the misery of Egypt to the land of the Canaanites, Hethites, Amorites, Perizzites, Hivites, and Jebusites—a land flowing with milk and honey. ¹⁸ They will listen to what you say. Then you, along with the elders of Israel, must go to the king of Egypt and say to him: The LORD, the God of the Hebrews, has met with us. Now please let us go on a three-day trip into the wilderness so that we may sacrifice to the LORD our God.

¹⁹ "However, I know that the king of Egypt will not allow you to go, even under force from a strong hand. ²⁰ But when I stretch out my hand and strike Egypt with all my miracles that I will perform in it, after that, he will let you go. ²¹ And

I will give these people such favor with the Egyptians that when you go, you will not go empty-handed. ²² Each woman will ask her neighbor and any woman staying in her house for silver and gold jewelry, and clothing, and you will put them on your sons and daughters. So you will plunder the Egyptians."

Exodus 4
Miraculous Signs for Moses

¹ Moses answered, "What if they won't believe me and will not obey me but say, 'The LORD did not appear to you'?"

² The LORD asked him, "What is that in your hand?"

"A staff," he replied.

³ "Throw it on the ground," he said. So Moses threw it on the ground, it became a snake, and he ran from it. ⁴ The LORD told Moses, "Stretch out your hand and grab it by the tail." So he stretched out his hand and caught it, and it became a staff in his hand. ⁵ "This will take place," he continued, "so that they will believe that the LORD, the God of their fathers, the God of Abraham, the God of Isaac, and the God of Jacob, has appeared to you."

⁶ In addition the LORD said to him, "Put your hand inside your cloak." So he put his hand inside his cloak, and when he took it out, his hand was diseased, resembling snow. ⁷ "Put your hand back inside your cloak," he said. So he put his hand back inside his cloak, and when he took it out, it had again become like the rest of his skin. ⁸ "If they will not believe you and will not respond to the evidence of the first sign, they may believe the evidence of the second sign. ⁹ And if they don't believe even these two signs or listen to what you say, take some water from the Nile and pour it on the dry ground. The water you take from the Nile will become blood on the ground."

"This is my name forever; this is how I am to be remembered in every generation." EXODUS 3:15

[10] But Moses replied to the Lord, "Please, Lord, I have never been eloquent—either in the past or recently or since you have been speaking to your servant—because my mouth and my tongue are sluggish."

[11] The Lord said to him, "Who placed a mouth on humans? Who makes a person mute or deaf, seeing or blind? Is it not I, the Lord? [12] Now go! I will help you speak and I will teach you what to say."

[13] Moses said, "Please, Lord, send someone else."

[14] Then the Lord's anger burned against Moses, and he said, "Isn't Aaron the Levite your brother? I know that he can speak well. And also, he is on his way now to meet you. He will rejoice when he sees you. [15] You will speak with him and tell him what to say. I will help both you and him to speak and will teach you both what to do. [16] He will speak to the people for you. He will serve as a mouth for you, and you will serve as God to him. [17] And take this staff in your hand that you will perform the signs with."

Moses's Return to Egypt

[18] Then Moses went back to his father-in-law Jethro and said to him, "Please let me return to my relatives in Egypt and see if they are still living."

Jethro said to Moses, "Go in peace."

[19] Now in Midian the Lord told Moses, "Return to Egypt, for all the men who wanted to kill you are dead." [20] So Moses took his wife and sons, put them on a donkey, and returned to the land of Egypt. And Moses took God's staff in his hand.

[21] The Lord instructed Moses, "When you go back to Egypt, make sure you do before Pharaoh all the wonders that I have put within your power. But I will harden his heart so that he won't let the people go. [22] And you will say to Pharaoh: This is what the Lord says: Israel is my firstborn son. [23] I told you: Let my son go so that he may worship me, but you refused to let him go. Look, I am about to kill your firstborn son!"

[24] On the trip, at an overnight campsite, it happened that the Lord confronted him and intended to put him to death. [25] So Zipporah took a flint, cut off her son's foreskin, threw it at Moses's feet, and said, "You are a bridegroom of blood to me!" [26] So he let him alone. At that time she said, "You are a bridegroom of blood," referring to the circumcision.

Reunion of Moses and Aaron

[27] Now the Lord had said to Aaron, "Go and meet Moses in the wilderness." So he went and met him at the mountain of God and kissed him. [28] Moses told Aaron everything the Lord had sent him to say, and about all the signs he had

commanded him to do. [29] Then Moses and Aaron went and assembled all the elders of the Israelites. [30] Aaron repeated everything the LORD had said to Moses and performed the signs before the people. [31] The people believed, and when they heard that the LORD had paid attention to them and that he had seen their misery, they knelt low and worshiped.

Joshua 5:13-15
Commander of the Lord's Army

[13] When Joshua was near Jericho, he looked up and saw a man standing in front of him with a drawn sword in his hand. Joshua approached him and asked, "Are you for us or for our enemies?"

[14] "Neither," he replied. "I have now come as commander of the LORD's army."

Then Joshua bowed with his face to the ground in worship and asked him, "What does my lord want to say to his servant?"

[15] The commander of the LORD's army said to Joshua, "Remove the sandals from your feet, for the place where you are standing is holy." And Joshua did that.

Matthew 22:23-33
The Sadducees and the Resurrection

[23] That same day some Sadducees, who say there is no resurrection, came up to him and questioned him: [24] "Teacher, Moses said, if a man dies, having no children, his brother is to marry his wife and raise up offspring for his brother. [25] Now there were seven brothers among us. The first got married and died. Having no offspring, he left his wife to his brother. [26] The same thing happened to the second also, and the third, and so on to all seven. [27] Last of all, the woman died. [28] In the resurrection, then, whose wife will she be of the seven? For they all had married her."

[29] Jesus answered them, "You are mistaken, because you don't know the Scriptures or the power of God. [30] For in the resurrection they neither marry nor are given in marriage but are like angels in heaven. [31] Now concerning the resurrection of the dead, haven't you read what was spoken to you by God: [32] I am the God of Abraham and the God of Isaac and the God of Jacob? He is not the God of the dead, but of the living."

[33] And when the crowds heard this, they were astonished at his teaching.

Day 5
The Lord Promises Freedom

Exodus 5

Moses Confronts Pharaoh

Later, Moses and Aaron went in and said to Pharaoh, "This is what the LORD, the God of Israel, says: Let my people go, so that they may hold a festival for me in the wilderness."

2 But Pharaoh responded, "Who is the LORD that I should obey him by letting Israel go? I don't know the LORD, and besides, I will not let Israel go."

3 They answered, "The God of the Hebrews has met with us. Please let us go on a three-day trip into the wilderness so that we may sacrifice to the LORD our God, or else he may strike us with plague or sword."

4 The king of Egypt said to them, "Moses and Aaron, why are you causing the people to neglect their work? Get to your labor!" 5 Pharaoh also said, "Look, the people of the land are so numerous, and you would stop them from their labor."

Further Oppression of Israel

6 That day Pharaoh commanded the overseers of the people as well as their foremen: 7 "Don't continue to supply the people with straw for making bricks, as before. They must go and gather straw for themselves. 8 But require the same quota of bricks from them as they were making before; do not reduce it. For they are slackers—that is why they are crying out, 'Let us go and sacrifice to our God.' 9 Impose heavier work on the men. Then they will be occupied with it and not pay attention to deceptive words."

10 So the overseers and foremen of the people went out and said to them, "This is what Pharaoh says: 'I am not giving you straw. 11 Go get straw yourselves wherever

you can find it, but there will be no reduction at all in your workload.'" ¹² So the people scattered throughout the land of Egypt to gather stubble for straw. ¹³ The overseers insisted, "Finish your assigned work each day, just as you did when straw was provided." ¹⁴ Then the Israelite foremen, whom Pharaoh's slave drivers had set over the people, were beaten and asked, "Why haven't you finished making your prescribed number of bricks yesterday or today, as you did before?"

¹⁵ So the Israelite foremen went in and cried for help to Pharaoh: "Why are you treating your servants this way? ¹⁶ No straw has been given to your servants, yet they say to us, 'Make bricks!' Look, your servants are being beaten, but it is your own people who are at fault."

¹⁷ But he said, "You are slackers. Slackers! That is why you are saying, 'Let us go sacrifice to the LORD.' ¹⁸ Now get to work. No straw will be given to you, but you must produce the same quantity of bricks."

¹⁹ The Israelite foremen saw that they were in trouble when they were told, "You cannot reduce your daily quota of bricks." ²⁰ When they left Pharaoh, they confronted Moses and Aaron, who stood waiting to meet them.

²¹ "May the LORD take note of you and judge," they said to them, "because you have made us reek to Pharaoh and his officials—putting a sword in their hand to kill us!"

²² So Moses went back to the LORD and asked, "Lord, why have you caused trouble for this people? And why did you ever send me? ²³ Ever since I went in to Pharaoh to speak in your name he has caused trouble for this people, and you haven't rescued your people at all."

Exodus 6:1-27

¹ But the LORD replied to Moses, "Now you will see what I will do to Pharaoh: because of a strong hand he will let them go, and because of a strong hand he will drive them from his land."

God Promises Freedom

² Then God spoke to Moses, telling him, "I am the LORD. ³ I appeared to Abraham, Isaac, and Jacob as God Almighty, but I was not known to them by my name 'the LORD.' ⁴ I also established my covenant with them to give them the land of Canaan, the land they lived in as aliens. ⁵ Furthermore, I have heard the groaning of the Israelites, whom the Egyptians are forcing to work as slaves, and I have remembered my covenant.

⁶ "Therefore tell the Israelites: I am the LORD, and I will bring you out from the forced labor of the Egyptians and rescue you from slavery to them. I will redeem

you with an outstretched arm and great acts of judgment. [7] I will take you as my people, and I will be your God. You will know that I am the LORD your God, who brought you out from the forced labor of the Egyptians. [8] I will bring you to the land that I swore to give to Abraham, Isaac, and Jacob, and I will give it to you as a possession. I am the LORD." [9] Moses told this to the Israelites, but they did not listen to him because of their broken spirit and hard labor.

[10] Then the LORD spoke to Moses, [11] "Go and tell Pharaoh king of Egypt to let the Israelites go from his land."

[12] But Moses said in the LORD's presence: "If the Israelites will not listen to me, then how will Pharaoh listen to me, since I am such a poor speaker?" [13] Then the LORD spoke to Moses and Aaron and gave them commands concerning both the Israelites and Pharaoh king of Egypt to bring the Israelites out of the land of Egypt.

Genealogy of Moses and Aaron

[14] These are the heads of their fathers' families:

The sons of Reuben, the firstborn of Israel:
Hanoch and Pallu, Hezron and Carmi.
These are the clans of Reuben.
[15] The sons of Simeon:
Jemuel, Jamin, Ohad, Jachin,
Zohar, and Shaul, the son of a Canaanite woman.
These are the clans of Simeon.
[16] These are the names of the sons of Levi
according to their family records;
Gershon, Kohath, and Merari.
Levi lived 137 years.
[17] The sons of Gershon:
Libni and Shimei, by their clans.
[18] The sons of Kohath:
Amram, Izhar, Hebron, and Uzziel.
Kohath lived 133 years.
[19] The sons of Merari:
Mahli and Mushi.
These are the clans of the Levites
according to their family records.
[20] Amram married his father's sister Jochebed,
and she bore him Aaron and Moses.
Amram lived 137 years.
[21] The sons of Izhar:
Korah, Nepheg, and Zichri.
[22] The sons of Uzziel:
Mishael, Elzaphan, and Sithri.

²³ Aaron married Elisheba,
daughter of Amminadab and sister of Nahshon.
She bore him Nadab and Abihu, Eleazar and Ithamar.
²⁴ The sons of Korah:
Assir, Elkanah, and Abiasaph.
These are the clans of the Korahites.
²⁵ Aaron's son Eleazar married
one of the daughters of Putiel,
and she bore him Phinehas.
These are the heads of the Levite families by their clans.

²⁶ It was this Aaron and Moses whom the LORD told, "Bring the Israelites out of the land of Egypt according to their military divisions." ²⁷ Moses and Aaron were the ones who spoke to Pharaoh king of Egypt in order to bring the Israelites out of Egypt.

Isaiah 6:4-5

⁴ The foundations of the doorways shook at the sound of their voices, and the temple was filled with smoke.

⁵ Then I said:

Woe is me for I am ruined
because I am a man of unclean lips
and live among a people of unclean lips,
and because my eyes have seen the King,
the LORD of Armies.

Psalm 68:4-6

⁴ Sing to God! Sing praises to his name.
Exalt him who rides on the clouds—
his name is the LORD—and celebrate before him.
⁵ God in his holy dwelling is
a father of the fatherless
and a champion of widows.
⁶ God provides homes for those who are deserted.
He leads out the prisoners to prosperity,
but the rebellious live in a scorched land.

Day 6
Grace Day

Use today to pray, rest, and reflect on this week's reading, giving thanks for the grace that is ours in Christ.

God in his holy dwelling is
a father of the fatherless
and a champion of widows.
God provides homes for those who are deserted.
He leads out the prisoners to prosperity,
but the rebellious live in a scorched land.

PSALM 68:5-6

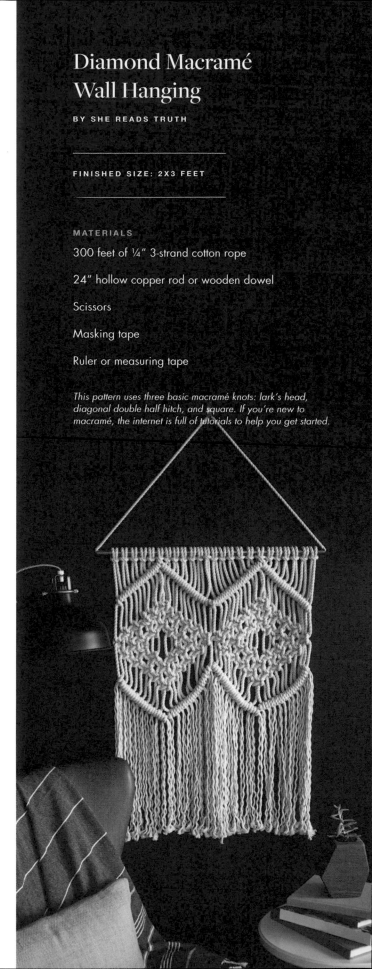

Diamond Macramé
Wall Hanging

BY SHE READS TRUTH

FINISHED SIZE: 2X3 FEET

MATERIALS

300 feet of ¼" 3-strand cotton rope

24" hollow copper rod or wooden dowel

Scissors

Masking tape

Ruler or measuring tape

This pattern uses three basic macramé knots: lark's head, diagonal double half hitch, and square. If you're new to macramé, the internet is full of tutorials to help you get started.

INSTRUCTIONS

1. Cut a 4-foot length of rope to hang your project. Thread the rope through the opening in your rod and knot, hiding the knot in the rod. Find a sturdy place to hang your project as you work.

2. Cut your remaining rope into twenty-four 12-foot cords. Wrap a piece of masking tape around the rope before each cut to keep cords from unraveling as you work.

3. Fold each cord in half and mount it to the rod using a **lark's head knot**. This gives you 48 individual cords to work with, numbered 1-48 from left to right.

4. Beginning with cords 12 and 13, tie a **diagonal double half hitch knot** in each set of cords, working from right to left until you reach cord 1. Each knot will be slightly lower than the previous one, eventually forming a 5-inch diagonal line from cord 13 to cord 1.

5. Return to cord 13. Tie a diagonal double half hitch knot in each pair of cords from left to right until you reach cord 24.

6. Move to cords 37 and 36. Leading with cord 37, tie diagonal double half hitch knots from right to left until you reach cord 24.

7. Return to cord 37 and tie diagonal double half hitch knots in the opposite direction, ending with cord 48.

8. Find cords 11-14 and and measure 4 inches from the knot at the center of this diamond. Mark across the four cords with a piece of masking tape to help keep the next section even. Repeat with cords 35-38.

Square knots in steps 9-19 are all 4-cord and begin with the cord noted.

9. Beginning with cord 11, tie one **square knot** using cords 11-14. Repeat with cords 35-38.

10. For the next row, begin with strand 9, tie 2 square knots, skip 16 cords, and tie 2 more square knots.

11. For the next row, begin with strand 7, tie 3 square knots, skip 12 cords, and tie 3 more square knots.

12. For the next row, begin with strand 5, tie 4 square knots, skip 8 cords, and tie 4 more square knots.

13. For the next row, begin with strand 3, tie 2 square knots, skip 4 cords, tie 2 square knots, skip 4 cords, tie 2 square knots, skip 4 cords, and finish with 2 square knots.

14. For the next row, begin with tying 2 square knots, skip 8 cords, and tie 4 square knots, skip 8 cords, and finish with 2 square knots. (This is the center of the two big diamonds.)

15. For the next row, begin with strand 3, tie 2 square knots, skip 4 cords, tie 2 square knots, skip 4 cords, tie 2 square knots, skip 4 cords, and finish with 2 square knots.

16. For the next row, begin with strand 5, tie 4 square knots, skip 8 cords, and tie 4 more square knots.

17. For the next row, begin with strand 7, tie 3 square knots, skip 12 cords, and tie 3 more square knots.

18. For the next row, begin with strand 9, tie 2 square knots, skip 16 cords, and tie 2 more square knots.

19. For the next row, begin with strand 11, tie 1 square knot, skip 20 cords, and tie 1 final square knot.

20. Repeat step 8, this time measuring 4 inches from the bottom of the last completed square knots on cords 1, 24, and 48.

21. Beginning with strand 1 and moving left to right, tie diagonal double half hitch knots until you reach cord 12.

22. Skip ahead to cord 24 and tie diagonal double half hitch knots in the opposite direction until you meet cord 12, knotting the last 2 cords together to complete the V shape.

23. Repeat steps 20 and 21, beginning with cords 25 and 48, respectively.

24. Measure 12 inches from the bottommost knot. Use masking tape to draw a straight line across the loose cords and cut along this line to make sure the bottom of your wall hanging is straight.

25. Unravel the remaining cords into their 3 strands to finish the piece.

Day 7
Weekly Truth

God replied to Moses, "I AM WHO I AM."

EXODUS 3:14

Scripture is God-breathed and true. When we memorize it, we carry the gospel with us wherever we go.

In this week's verse, God reveals the greatness of His power through the authority of His name.

Find the corresponding memory card in the back of your book.

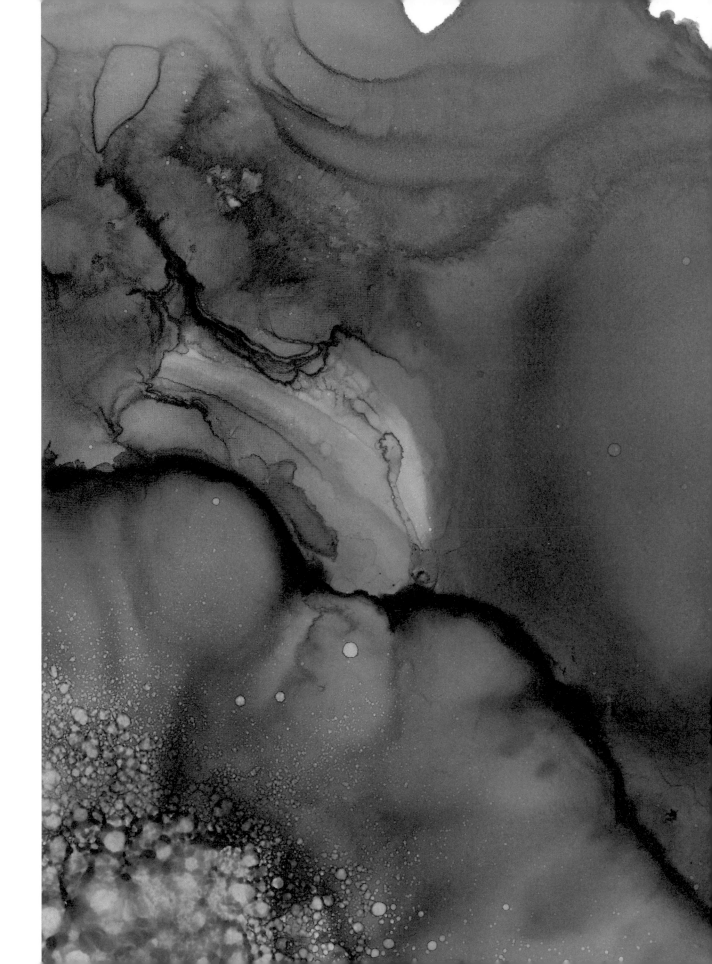

Day 8
The Plagues Begin

Exodus 6:28-30
Moses and Aaron Before Pharaoh

n the day the Lord spoke to Moses in the land of Egypt, [29] he said to him, "I am the Lord; tell Pharaoh king of Egypt everything I am telling you."

[30] But Moses replied in the Lord's presence, "Since I am such a poor speaker, how will Pharaoh listen to me?"

Exodus 7

[1] The Lord answered Moses, "See, I have made you like God to Pharaoh, and Aaron your brother will be your prophet. [2] You must say whatever I command you; then Aaron your brother must declare it to Pharaoh so that he will let the Israelites go from his land. [3] But I will harden Pharaoh's heart and multiply my signs and wonders in the land of Egypt. [4] Pharaoh will not listen to you, but I will put my hand into Egypt and bring the military divisions of my people the Israelites out of the land of Egypt by great acts of judgment. [5] The Egyptians will know that I am the Lord when I stretch out my hand against Egypt and bring out the Israelites from among them."

[6] So Moses and Aaron did this; they did just as the Lord commanded them. [7] Moses was eighty years old and Aaron eighty-three when they spoke to Pharaoh.

[8] The Lord said to Moses and Aaron, [9] "When Pharaoh tells you, 'Perform a miracle,' tell Aaron, 'Take your staff and throw it down before Pharaoh. It will become a serpent.'" [10] So Moses and Aaron went in to Pharaoh and did just as the Lord had commanded. Aaron threw down his staff before Pharaoh and his officials, and it became a serpent. [11] But then Pharaoh called the wise men and sorcerers—the magicians of Egypt, and they also did the same thing by their occult practices.

¹² Each one threw down his staff, and it became a serpent. But Aaron's staff swallowed their staffs. ¹³ However, Pharaoh's heart was hard, and he did not listen to them, as the LORD had said.

The First Plague: Water Turned to Blood

¹⁴ Then the LORD said to Moses, "Pharaoh's heart is hard: He refuses to let the people go. ¹⁵ Go to Pharaoh in the morning. When you see him walking out to the water, stand ready to meet him by the bank of the Nile. Take in your hand the staff that turned into a snake. ¹⁶ Tell him: The LORD, the God of the Hebrews, has sent me to tell you: Let my people go, so that they may worship me in the wilderness, but so far you have not listened. ¹⁷ This is what the LORD says: Here is how you will know that I am the LORD. Watch. I am about to strike the water in the Nile with the staff in my hand, and it will turn to blood. ¹⁸ The fish in the Nile will die, the river will stink, and the Egyptians will be unable to drink water from it."

¹⁹ So the LORD said to Moses, "Tell Aaron: Take your staff and stretch out your hand over the waters of Egypt—over their rivers, canals, ponds, and all their water reservoirs—and they will become blood. There will be blood throughout the land of Egypt, even in wooden and stone containers."

²⁰ Moses and Aaron did just as the LORD had commanded; in the sight of Pharaoh and his officials, he raised the staff and struck the water in the Nile, and all the water in the Nile was turned to blood. ²¹ The fish in the Nile died, and the river smelled so bad the Egyptians could not drink water from it. There was blood throughout the land of Egypt.

²² But the magicians of Egypt did the same thing by their occult practices. So Pharaoh's heart was hard, and he would not listen to them, as the LORD had said. ²³ Pharaoh turned around, went into his palace, and didn't take even this to heart. ²⁴ All the Egyptians dug around the Nile for water to drink because they could not drink the water from the river. ²⁵ Seven days passed after the LORD struck the Nile.

Exodus 8
The Second Plague: Frogs

¹ Then the LORD said to Moses, "Go in to Pharaoh and tell him: This is what the LORD says: Let my people go, so that they may worship me. ² But if you refuse to let them go, then I will plague all your territory with frogs. ³ The Nile will swarm with frogs; they will come up and go into your palace, into your bedroom and on your bed, into the houses of your officials and your people, and into your ovens and kneading bowls. ⁴ The frogs will come up on you, your people, and all your officials."

⁵ The LORD then said to Moses, "Tell Aaron: Stretch out your hand with your staff over the rivers, canals, and ponds, and cause the frogs to come up onto the land of Egypt." ⁶ When Aaron stretched out his hand over the waters of Egypt, the frogs came up and covered the land of Egypt. ⁷ But the magicians did the same thing by their occult practices and brought frogs up onto the land of Egypt.

⁸ Pharaoh summoned Moses and Aaron and said, "Appeal to the LORD to remove the frogs from me and my people. Then I will let the people go and they can sacrifice to the LORD."

⁹ Moses said to Pharaoh, "You may have the honor of choosing. When should I appeal on behalf of you, your officials, and your people, that the frogs be taken away from you and your houses, and remain only in the Nile?"

¹⁰ "Tomorrow," he answered.

Moses replied, "As you have said, so that you may know there is no one like the LORD our God,

Pharaoh's heart was hard, and he did not listen to them, as the LORD had said. EXODUS 7:13

[11] the frogs will go away from you, your houses, your officials, and your people. The frogs will remain only in the Nile." [12] After Moses and Aaron went out from Pharaoh, Moses cried out to the LORD for help concerning the frogs that he had brought against Pharaoh. [13] The LORD did as Moses had said: the frogs in the houses, courtyards, and fields died. [14] They piled them in countless heaps, and there was a terrible odor in the land. [15] But when Pharaoh saw there was relief, he hardened his heart and would not listen to them, as the LORD had said.

The Third Plague: Gnats

[16] Then the LORD said to Moses, "Tell Aaron: Stretch out your staff and strike the dust of the land, and it will become gnats throughout the land of Egypt." [17] And they did this. Aaron stretched out his hand with his staff, and when he struck the dust of the land, gnats were on people and animals. All the dust of the land became gnats throughout the land of Egypt. [18] The magicians tried to produce gnats using their occult practices, but they could not. The gnats remained on people and animals.

[19] "This is the finger of God," the magicians said to Pharaoh. But Pharaoh's heart was hard, and he would not listen to them, as the LORD had said.

The Fourth Plague: Swarms of Flies

[20] The LORD said to Moses, "Get up early in the morning and present yourself to Pharaoh when you see him going out to the water. Tell him: This is what the LORD says: Let my people go, so that they may worship me. [21] But if you will not let my people go, then I will send swarms of flies against you, your officials, your people, and your houses. The Egyptians' houses will swarm with flies, and so will the land where they live.

[22] But on that day I will give special treatment to the land of Goshen, where my people are living;

no flies will be there. This way you will know that I, the LORD, am in the land. [23] I will make a distinction between my people and your people. This sign will take place tomorrow."

[24] And the LORD did this. Thick swarms of flies went into Pharaoh's palace and his officials' houses. Throughout Egypt the land was ruined because of the swarms of flies. [25] Then Pharaoh summoned Moses and Aaron and said, "Go sacrifice to your God within the country."

[26] But Moses said, "It would not be right to do that, because what we will sacrifice to the LORD our God is detestable to the Egyptians. If we sacrifice what the Egyptians detest in front of them, won't they stone us? [27] We must go a distance of three days into the wilderness and sacrifice to the LORD our God as he instructs us."

²⁸ Pharaoh responded, "I will let you go and sacrifice to the LORD your God in the wilderness, but don't go very far. Make an appeal for me."

²⁹ "As soon as I leave you," Moses said, "I will appeal to the LORD, and tomorrow the swarms of flies will depart from Pharaoh, his officials, and his people. But Pharaoh must not act deceptively again by refusing to let the people go and sacrifice to the LORD." ³⁰ Then Moses left Pharaoh's presence and appealed to the LORD. ³¹ The LORD did as Moses had said: He removed the swarms of flies from Pharaoh, his officials, and his people; not one was left. ³² But Pharaoh hardened his heart this time also and did not let the people go.

Genesis 47:4-6

⁴ And they said to Pharaoh, "We have come to stay in the land for a while because there is no grazing land for your servants' sheep, since the famine in the land of Canaan has been severe. So now, please let your servants settle in the land of Goshen."

⁵ Then Pharaoh said to Joseph, "Now that your father and brothers have come to you, ⁶ the land of Egypt is open before you; settle your father and brothers in the best part of the land. They can live in the land of Goshen. If you know of any capable men among them, put them in charge of my livestock."

Psalm 95:1-5
Worship and Warning

¹ Come, let us shout joyfully to the LORD,
shout triumphantly to the rock of our salvation!
² Let us enter his presence with thanksgiving;
let us shout triumphantly to him in song.

³ For the LORD is a great God,
a great King above all gods.
⁴ The depths of the earth are in his hand,
and the mountain peaks are his.
⁵ The sea is his; he made it.
His hands formed the dry land.

Day 9
The Plagues Continue

Exodus 9

The Fifth Plague: Death of Livestock

Then the Lord said to Moses, "Go in to Pharaoh and say to him: This is what the Lord, the God of the Hebrews, says: Let my people go, so that they may worship me. ² But if you refuse to let them go and keep holding them, ³ then the Lord's hand will bring a severe plague against your livestock in the field—the horses, donkeys, camels, herds, and flocks. ⁴ But the Lord will make a distinction between the livestock of Israel and the livestock of Egypt, so that nothing of all that the Israelites own will die." ⁵ And the Lord set a time, saying, "Tomorrow the Lord will do this thing in the land." ⁶ The Lord did this the next day. All the Egyptian livestock died, but none among the Israelite livestock died. ⁷ Pharaoh sent messengers who saw that not a single one of the Israelite livestock was dead. But Pharaoh's heart was hard, and he did not let the people go.

The Sixth Plague: Boils

⁸ Then the Lord said to Moses and Aaron, "Take handfuls of furnace soot, and Moses is to throw it toward heaven in the sight of Pharaoh. ⁹ It will become fine dust over the entire land of Egypt. It will become festering boils on people and animals throughout the land of Egypt." ¹⁰ So they took furnace soot and stood before Pharaoh. Moses threw it toward heaven, and it became festering boils on people and animals. ¹¹ The magicians could not stand before Moses because of the boils, for the boils were on the magicians as well as on all the Egyptians. ¹² But the Lord hardened Pharaoh's heart and he did not listen to them, as the Lord had told Moses.

The Seventh Plague: Hail

¹³ Then the Lord said to Moses, "Get up early in the morning and present yourself to Pharaoh. Tell him: This is what the Lord, the God of the Hebrews says: Let my people go, so that they may worship me. ¹⁴ For this time I am about to send all my

plagues against you, your officials, and your people. Then you will know there is no one like me on the whole earth. ¹⁵ By now I could have stretched out my hand and struck you and your people with a plague, and you would have been obliterated from the earth. ¹⁶ However, I have let you live for this purpose: to show you my power and to make my name known on the whole earth. ¹⁷ You are still acting arrogantly against my people by not letting them go. ¹⁸ Tomorrow at this time I will rain down the worst hail that has ever occurred in Egypt from the day it was founded until now. ¹⁹ Therefore give orders to bring your livestock and all that you have in the field into shelters. Every person and animal that is in the field and not brought inside will die when the hail falls on them." ²⁰ Those among Pharaoh's officials who feared the word of the Lord made their servants and livestock flee to shelters, ²¹ but those who didn't take to heart the Lord's word left their servants and livestock in the field.

²² Then the Lord said to Moses, "Stretch out your hand toward heaven and let there be hail throughout the land of Egypt—on people and animals and every plant of the field in the land of Egypt." ²³ So Moses stretched out his staff toward heaven, and the Lord sent thunder and hail. Lightning struck the land, and the Lord rained hail on the land of Egypt. ²⁴ The hail, with lightning flashing through it, was so severe that nothing like it had occurred in the land of Egypt since it had become a nation. ²⁵ Throughout the land of Egypt, the hail struck down everything in the field, both people and animals. The hail beat down every plant of the field and shattered every tree in the field. ²⁶ The only place it didn't hail was in the land of Goshen, where the Israelites were.

²⁷ Pharaoh sent for Moses and Aaron. "I have sinned this time," he said to them. "The Lord is the righteous one, and I and my people are the guilty ones. ²⁸ Make an appeal to the Lord. There has been enough of God's thunder and hail. I will let you go; you don't need to stay any longer."

²⁹ Moses said to him, "When I have left the city, I will spread out my hands to the Lord. The thunder will cease, and there will be no more hail, so that you may know the earth belongs to the Lord. ³⁰ But as for you and your officials, I know that you still do not fear the Lord God."

³¹ The flax and the barley were destroyed because the barley was ripe and the flax was budding, ³² but the wheat and the spelt were not destroyed since they are later crops.

³³ Moses left Pharaoh and the city, and spread out his hands to the Lord. Then the thunder and hail ceased, and rain no longer poured down on the land. ³⁴ When Pharaoh saw that the rain, hail, and thunder had ceased, he sinned again and hardened his heart, he and his officials. ³⁵ So Pharaoh's heart was hard, and he did not let the Israelites go, as the Lord had said through Moses.

"Then you will know there is no one like me on the whole earth." EXODUS 9:14

Exodus 10

The Eighth Plague: Locusts

¹ Then the LORD said to Moses, "Go to Pharaoh, for I have hardened his heart and the hearts of his officials so that I may do these miraculous signs of mine among them, ² and so that you may tell your son and grandson how severely I dealt with the Egyptians and performed miraculous signs among them, and you will know that I am the LORD."

³ So Moses and Aaron went in to Pharaoh and told him, "This is what the LORD, the God of the Hebrews, says: How long will you refuse to humble yourself before me? Let my people go, that they may worship me. ⁴ But if you refuse to let my people go, then tomorrow I will bring locusts into your territory. ⁵ They will cover the surface of the land so that no one will be able to see the land. They will eat the remainder left to you that escaped the hail; they will eat every tree you have growing in the fields. ⁶ They will fill your houses, all your officials' houses, and the houses of all the Egyptians—something your fathers and grandfathers never saw since the time they occupied the land until today." Then he turned and left Pharaoh's presence.

⁷ Pharaoh's officials asked him, "How long must this man be a snare to us? Let the men go, so that they may worship the LORD their God. Don't you realize yet that Egypt is devastated?"

⁸ So Moses and Aaron were brought back to Pharaoh. "Go, worship the LORD your God," Pharaoh said. "But exactly who will be going?"

⁹ Moses replied, "We will go with our young and with our old; we will go with our sons and with our daughters, with our flocks and with our herds because we must hold the LORD's festival."

¹⁰ He said to them, "The Lord would have to be with you if I would ever let you and your families go! Look out—you're heading for trouble. ¹¹ No, go—just able-bodied men—worship the LORD, since that's what you want." And they were driven from Pharaoh's presence.

¹² The LORD then said to Moses, "Stretch out your hand over the land of Egypt, and the locusts will come up over it and eat every plant in the land, everything that the hail left." ¹³ So Moses stretched out his staff over the land of Egypt, and the LORD sent an east wind over the land all that day and through the night. By morning the east wind had brought in the locusts. ¹⁴ The locusts went up over the entire land of Egypt and settled on the whole territory of Egypt. Never before had there been such a large number of locusts, and there never will be again. ¹⁵ They covered the surface of the whole land so that the land was black, and they

consumed all the plants on the ground and all the fruit on the trees that the hail had left. Nothing green was left on the trees or the plants in the field throughout the land of Egypt.

16 Pharaoh urgently sent for Moses and Aaron and said, "I have sinned against the LORD your God and against you. 17 Please forgive my sin once more and make an appeal to the LORD your God, so that he will just take this death away from me." 18 Moses left Pharaoh's presence and appealed to the LORD. 19 Then the LORD changed the wind to a strong west wind, and it carried off the locusts and blew them into the Red Sea. Not a single locust was left in all the territory of Egypt. 20 But the LORD hardened Pharaoh's heart, and he did not let the Israelites go.

The Ninth Plague: Darkness

21 Then the LORD said to Moses, "Stretch out your hand toward heaven, and there will be darkness over the land of Egypt, a darkness that can be felt." 22 So Moses stretched out his hand toward heaven, and there was thick darkness throughout the land of Egypt for three days. 23 One person could not see another, and for three days they did not move from where they were. Yet all the Israelites had light where they lived.

24 Pharaoh summoned Moses and said, "Go, worship the LORD. Even your families may go with you; only your flocks and herds must stay behind."

25 Moses responded, "You must also let us have sacrifices and burnt offerings to prepare for the LORD our God. 26 Even our livestock must go with us; not a hoof will be left behind because we will take some of them to worship the LORD our God. We will not know what we will use to worship the LORD until we get there."

27 But the LORD hardened Pharaoh's heart, and he was unwilling to let them go. 28 Pharaoh said to him, "Leave me! Make sure you never see my face again, for on the day you see my face, you will die."

29 "As you have said," Moses replied,

"I will never see your face again."

Exodus 11

The Tenth Plague: Death of the Firstborn

1 The LORD said to Moses, "I will bring one more plague on Pharaoh and on Egypt. After that, he will let you go from here. When he lets you go, he will drive you out of here. 2 Now announce to the people that both men and women should ask

their neighbors for silver and gold items." ³ The Lord gave the people favor with the Egyptians. In addition, Moses himself was very highly regarded in the land of Egypt by Pharaoh's officials and the people.

⁴ So Moses said, "This is what the Lord says: About midnight I will go throughout Egypt, ⁵ and every firstborn male in the land of Egypt will die, from the firstborn of Pharaoh who sits on his throne to the firstborn of the servant girl who is at the grindstones, as well as every firstborn of the livestock. ⁶ Then there will be a great cry of anguish through all the land of Egypt such as never was before or ever will be again. ⁷ But against all the Israelites, whether people or animals, not even a dog will snarl, so that you may know that the Lord makes a distinction between Egypt and Israel. ⁸ All these officials of yours will come down to me and bow before me, saying: Get out, you and all the people who follow you. After that, I will get out." And he went out from Pharaoh's presence fiercely angry.

⁹ The Lord said to Moses, "Pharaoh will not listen to you, so that my wonders may be multiplied in the land of Egypt." ¹⁰ Moses and Aaron did all these wonders before Pharaoh, but the Lord hardened Pharaoh's heart, and he would not let the Israelites go out of his land.

Deuteronomy 7:6-11

⁶ For you are a holy people belonging to the Lord your God. The Lord your God has chosen you to be his own possession out of all the peoples on the face of the earth.

⁷ "The Lord had his heart set on you and chose you,

not because you were more numerous than all peoples, for you were the fewest of all peoples. ⁸ But because the Lord loved you and kept the oath he swore to your fathers, he brought you out with a strong hand and redeemed you from the place of slavery, from the power of Pharaoh king of Egypt. ⁹ Know that the Lord your God is God, the faithful God who keeps his gracious covenant loyalty for a thousand generations with those who love him and keep his commands. ¹⁰ But he directly pays back and destroys those who hate him. He will not hesitate to pay back directly the one who hates him. ¹¹ So keep the command—the statutes and ordinances—that I am giving you to follow today."

Romans 9:17

For the Scripture tells Pharaoh, I raised you up for this reason so that I may display my power in you and that my name may be proclaimed in the whole earth.

Month   Day

Day 10
The Passover

Exodus 12

Instructions for the Passover

The Lord said to Moses and Aaron in the land of Egypt: [2] "This month is to be the beginning of months for you; it is the first month of your year. [3] Tell the whole community of Israel that on the tenth day of this month they must each select an animal of the flock according to their fathers' families, one animal per family. [4] If the household is too small for a whole animal, that person and the neighbor nearest his house are to select one based on the combined number of people; you should apportion the animal according to what each will eat. [5] You must have an unblemished animal, a year-old male; you may take it from either the sheep or the goats. [6] You are to keep it until the fourteenth day of this month; then the whole assembly of the community of Israel will slaughter the animals at twilight. [7] They must take some of the blood and put it on the two doorposts and the lintel of the houses where they eat them. [8] They are to eat the meat that night; they should eat it, roasted over the fire along with unleavened bread and bitter herbs. [9] Do not eat any of it raw or cooked in boiling water, but only roasted over fire—its head as well as its legs and inner organs. [10] You must not leave any of it until morning; any part of it left until morning you must burn. [11] Here is how you must eat it: You must be dressed for travel, your sandals on your feet, and your staff in your hand. You are to eat it in a hurry; it is the Lord's Passover.

[12] "I will pass through the land of Egypt on that night and strike every firstborn male in the land of Egypt, both people and animals. I am the Lord; I will execute judgments against all the gods of Egypt. [13] The blood on the houses where you are staying will be a distinguishing mark for you; when I see the blood, I will pass over you. No plague will be among you to destroy you when I strike the land of Egypt.

14 "This day is to be a memorial for you, and you must celebrate it as a festival to the Lord. You are to celebrate it throughout your generations as a permanent statute. 15 You must eat unleavened bread for seven days. On the first day you must remove yeast from your houses. Whoever eats what is leavened from the first day through the seventh day must be cut off from Israel. 16 You are to hold a sacred assembly on the first day and another sacred assembly on the seventh day. No work may be done on those days except for preparing what people need to eat—you may do only that.

17 "You are to observe the Festival of Unleavened Bread because on this very day I brought your military divisions out of the land of Egypt. You must observe this day throughout your generations as a permanent statute. 18 You are to eat unleavened bread in the first month, from the evening of the fourteenth day of the month until the evening of the twenty-first day. 19 Yeast must not be found in your houses for seven days. If anyone eats something leavened, that person, whether a resident alien or native of the land, must be cut off from the community of Israel. 20 Do not eat anything leavened; eat unleavened bread in all your homes."

21 Then Moses summoned all the elders of Israel and said to them, "Go, select an animal from the flock according to your families, and slaughter the Passover animal. 22 Take a cluster of hyssop, dip it in the blood that is in the basin, and brush the lintel and the two doorposts with some of the blood in the basin. None of you may go out the door of his house until morning. 23 When the Lord passes through to strike Egypt and sees the blood on the lintel and the two doorposts, he will pass over the door and not let the destroyer enter your houses to strike you.

24 "Keep this command permanently as a statute for you and your descendants. 25 When you enter the land that the Lord will give you as he promised, you are to observe this ceremony. 26 When your children ask you, 'What does this ceremony mean to you?' 27 you are to reply, 'It is the Passover sacrifice to the Lord, for he passed over the houses of the Israelites in Egypt when he struck the Egyptians and spared our homes.'" So the people knelt low and worshiped. 28 Then the Israelites went and did this; they did just as the Lord had commanded Moses and Aaron.

The Exodus

29 Now at midnight the Lord struck every firstborn male in the land of Egypt, from the firstborn of Pharaoh who sat on his throne to the firstborn of the prisoner who was in the dungeon, and every firstborn of the livestock. 30 During the night Pharaoh got up, he along with all his officials and all the Egyptians, and there was a loud wailing throughout Egypt because there wasn't a house without someone dead. 31 He summoned Moses and Aaron during the night and said, "Get out immediately from among my people, both you and the Israelites, and go, worship the Lord as you have said. 32 Take even your flocks and your herds as you asked and leave, and also bless me."

33 Now the Egyptians pressured the people in order to send them quickly out of the country, for they said, "We're all going to die!" 34 So the people took their dough before it was leavened, with their kneading bowls wrapped up in their clothes on their shoulders.

35 The Israelites acted on Moses's word and asked the Egyptians for silver and gold items and for clothing. 36 And the Lord gave the people such favor with the Egyptians that they gave them what they requested. In this way they plundered the Egyptians.

37 The Israelites traveled from Rameses to Succoth, about six hundred thousand able-bodied men on foot, besides their families. 38 A mixed crowd also went up with them, along with a huge number of livestock, both flocks and herds. 39 The people

"The blood on the houses where you are staying will be a distinguishing mark for you; when I see the blood, I will pass over you." EXODUS 12:13

baked the dough they had brought out of Egypt into unleavened loaves, since it had no yeast; for when they were driven out of Egypt, they could not delay and had not prepared provisions for themselves.

[40] The time that the Israelites lived in Egypt was 430 years. [41] At the end of 430 years, on that same day, all the Lord's military divisions went out from the land of Egypt. [42] It was a night of vigil in honor of the Lord, because he would bring them out of the land of Egypt. This same night is in honor of the Lord, a night vigil for all the Israelites throughout their generations.

Passover Instruction

[43] The Lord said to Moses and Aaron, "This is the statute of the Passover: no foreigner may eat it. [44] But any slave a man has purchased may eat it, after you have circumcised him. [45] A temporary resident or hired worker may not eat the Passover. [46] It is to be eaten in one house. You may not take any of the meat outside the house, and you may not break any of its bones. [47] The whole community of Israel must celebrate it. [48] If an alien resides among you and wants to observe the Lord's Passover, every male in his household must be circumcised, and then he may participate; he will become like a native of the land. But no uncircumcised person may eat it. [49] The same law will apply to both the native and the alien who resides among you."

[50] Then all the Israelites did this; they did just as the Lord had commanded Moses and Aaron. [51] On that same day the Lord brought the Israelites out of the land of Egypt according to their military divisions.

Exodus 13:1-16

[1] The Lord spoke to Moses: [2] "Consecrate every firstborn male to me, the firstborn from every womb among the Israelites, both man and domestic animal; it is mine."

[3] Then Moses said to the people, "Remember this day when you came out of Egypt, out of the place of slavery, for the Lord brought you out of here by the strength of his hand. Nothing leavened may be eaten. [4] Today, in the month of Abib, you are going out. [5] When the Lord brings you into the land of the Canaanites, Hethites, Amorites, Hivites, and Jebusites, which he swore to your fathers that he would give you, a land flowing with milk and honey, you must carry out this ceremony in this month. [6] For seven days you must eat unleavened bread, and on the seventh day there is to be a festival to the Lord. [7] Unleavened bread is to be eaten for those seven days. Nothing leavened may be found among you, and no yeast may be found among you in all your territory. [8] On that day explain to your son, 'This is because of what the Lord did for me when I came out of Egypt.' [9] Let it serve as a sign for you on your hand and as a reminder on your forehead, so that the Lord's instruction may be in your mouth; for the Lord brought you out of Egypt with a strong hand. [10] Keep this statute at its appointed time from year to year.

[11] "When the LORD brings you into the land of the Canaanites, as he swore to you and your fathers, and gives it to you, [12] you are to present to the LORD every firstborn male of the womb. All firstborn offspring of the livestock you own that are males will be the LORD's. [13] You must redeem every firstborn of a donkey with a flock animal, but if you do not redeem it, break its neck. However, you must redeem every firstborn among your sons.

[14] "In the future, when your son asks you, 'What does this mean?' say to him, 'By the strength of his hand the LORD brought us out of Egypt, out of the place of slavery. [15] When Pharaoh stubbornly refused to let us go, the LORD killed every firstborn male in the land of Egypt, both the firstborn of humans and the firstborn of livestock. That is why I sacrifice to the LORD all the firstborn of the womb that are males, but I redeem all the firstborn of my sons.' [16] So let it be a sign on your hand and a symbol on your forehead, for the LORD brought us out of Egypt by the strength of his hand."

Psalm 51:7

Purify me with hyssop, and I will be clean;
wash me, and I will be whiter than snow.

John 1:29

The next day John saw Jesus coming toward him and said,

"Here is the Lamb of God, who takes away the sin of the world!"

Hymn
He Leadeth Me

Text: Joseph H. Gilmore, 1862
Tune: William B. Bradbury, 1864

He leadeth me: O blessed thought!
O words with heavenly comfort fraught!
Whate'er I do, where'er I be,
still 'tis God's hand that leadeth me.

Refrain:
He leadeth me, He leadeth me;
by His own hand He leadeth me:
His faithful follower I would be,
for by His hand He leadeth me.

Sometimes mid scenes of deepest gloom,
sometimes where Eden's flowers bloom,
by waters calm, o'er troubled sea,
still 'tis God's hand that leadeth me. *Refrain*

Lord, I would clasp Thy hand in mine,
nor ever murmur nor repine;
content, whatever lot I see,
since 'tis my God that leadeth me. *Refrain*

And when my task on earth is done,
when, by thy grace, the victory's won,
e'en death's cold wave I will not flee,
since God through Jordan leadeth me. *Refrain*

Day 11
Escape Through the Red Sea

Exodus 13:17-22
The Route of the Exodus

When Pharaoh let the people go, God did not lead them along the road to the land of the Philistines, even though it was nearby; for God said, "The people will change their minds and return to Egypt if they face war." ¹⁸ So he led the people around toward the Red Sea along the road of the wilderness. And the Israelites left the land of Egypt in battle formation.

¹⁹ Moses took the bones of Joseph with him, because Joseph had made the Israelites swear a solemn oath, saying, "God will certainly come to your aid; then you must take my bones with you from this place."

²⁰ They set out from Succoth and camped at Etham on the edge of the wilderness. ²¹ The Lord went ahead of them in a pillar of cloud to lead them on their way during the day and in a pillar of fire to give them light at night, so that they could travel day or night. ²² The pillar of cloud by day and the pillar of fire by night never left its place in front of the people.

Exodus 14

¹ Then the Lord spoke to Moses: ² "Tell the Israelites to turn back and camp in front of Pi-hahiroth, between Migdol and the sea; you must camp in front of Baal-zephon, facing it by the sea. ³ Pharaoh will say of the Israelites: They are wandering around the land in confusion; the wilderness has boxed them in. ⁴ I will harden Pharaoh's heart so that he will pursue them. Then I will receive glory by means of Pharaoh and all his army, and the Egyptians will know that I am the Lord." So the Israelites did this.

The Egyptian Pursuit

5 When the king of Egypt was told that the people had fled, Pharaoh and his officials changed their minds about the people and said: "What have we done? We have released Israel from serving us." 6 So he got his chariot ready and took his troops with him; 7 he took six hundred of the best chariots and all the rest of the chariots of Egypt, with officers in each one. 8 The Lord hardened the heart of Pharaoh king of Egypt, and he pursued the Israelites, who were going out defiantly. 9 The Egyptians—all Pharaoh's horses and chariots, his horsemen, and his army—chased after them and caught up with them as they camped by the sea beside Pi-hahiroth, in front of Baal-zephon.

10 As Pharaoh approached, the Israelites looked up and there were the Egyptians coming after them! The Israelites were terrified and cried out to the Lord for help. 11 They said to Moses: "Is it because there are no graves in Egypt that you have taken us away to die in the wilderness? What have you done to us by bringing us out of Egypt? 12 Isn't this what we told you in Egypt: Leave us alone so that we may serve the Egyptians? It would have been better for us to serve the Egyptians than to die in the wilderness."

13 But Moses said to the people, "Don't be afraid. Stand firm and see the Lord's salvation that he will accomplish for you today; for the Egyptians you see today, you will never see again. 14 The Lord will fight for you, and you must be quiet."

Escape Through the Red Sea

15 The Lord said to Moses, "Why are you crying out to me? Tell the Israelites to break camp. 16 As for you, lift up your staff, stretch out your hand over the sea, and divide it so that the Israelites can go through the sea on dry ground. 17 As for me, I am going to harden the hearts of the Egyptians so that they will go in after them, and I will receive glory by means of Pharaoh, all his army, and his chariots and horsemen. 18 The Egyptians will know

that I am the Lord when I receive glory through Pharaoh, his chariots, and his horsemen."

19 Then the angel of God, who was going in front of the Israelite forces, moved and went behind them. The pillar of cloud moved from in front of them and stood behind them. 20 It came between the Egyptian and Israelite forces. There was cloud and darkness, it lit up the night, and neither group came near the other all night long.

21 Then Moses stretched out his hand over the sea. The Lord drove the sea back with a powerful east wind all that night and turned the sea into dry land. So the waters were divided, 22 and the Israelites went through the sea on dry ground, with the waters like a wall to them on their right and their left.

23 The Egyptians set out in pursuit—all Pharaoh's horses, his chariots, and his horsemen—and went into the sea after them. 24 During the morning watch, the Lord looked down at the Egyptian forces from the pillar of fire and cloud, and threw the Egyptian forces into confusion. 25 He caused their chariot wheels to swerve and made them drive with difficulty. "Let's get away from Israel," the Egyptians said, "because the Lord is fighting for them against Egypt!"

26 Then the Lord said to Moses, "Stretch out your hand over the sea so that the water may come back on the Egyptians, on their chariots and horsemen." 27 So Moses stretched out his hand over the sea, and at daybreak the sea returned to its normal depth. While the Egyptians were trying to escape from it, the Lord threw them into the sea. 28 The water came back and covered the chariots and horsemen, plus the entire army of Pharaoh that had gone after them into the sea. Not even one of them survived.

29 But the Israelites had walked through the sea on dry ground, with the waters like a wall to them on

The pillar of cloud by day and the pillar of fire by night never left its place in front of the people. EXODUS 13:22

their right and their left. ³⁰ That day the LORD saved Israel from the power of the Egyptians, and Israel saw the Egyptians dead on the seashore. ³¹ When Israel saw the great power that the LORD used against the Egyptians, the people feared the LORD and believed in him and in his servant Moses.

Exodus 15:1-21
Israel's Song

¹ Then Moses and the Israelites sang this song to the LORD. They said:

I will sing to the LORD,
for he is highly exalted;
he has thrown the horse
and its rider into the sea.

² The LORD is my strength and my song; he has become my salvation.

This is my God, and I will praise him,
my father's God, and I will exalt him.
³ The LORD is a warrior;
the LORD is his name.

⁴ He threw Pharaoh's chariots
and his army into the sea;
the elite of his officers
were drowned in the Red Sea.
⁵ The floods covered them;
they sank to the depths like a stone.
⁶ LORD, your right hand is glorious in power.
LORD, your right hand shattered the enemy.
⁷ You overthrew your adversaries
by your great majesty.
You unleashed your burning wrath;
it consumed them like stubble.
⁸ The water heaped up at the blast from your nostrils;
the currents stood firm like a dam.
The watery depths congealed in the heart of the sea.
⁹ The enemy said:
"I will pursue, I will overtake,
I will divide the spoil.
My desire will be gratified at their expense.
I will draw my sword;
my hand will destroy them."

¹⁰ But you blew with your breath,
and the sea covered them.
They sank like lead
in the mighty waters.

¹¹ Lord, who is like you among the gods?
Who is like you, glorious in holiness,
revered with praises, performing wonders?
¹² You stretched out your right hand,
and the earth swallowed them.
¹³ With your faithful love,
you will lead the people
you have redeemed;
you will guide them to your holy dwelling
with your strength.

¹⁴ When the peoples hear, they will shudder;
anguish will seize the inhabitants of Philistia.
¹⁵ Then the chiefs of Edom will be terrified;
trembling will seize the leaders of Moab;
all the inhabitants of Canaan will panic;
¹⁶ terror and dread will fall on them.
They will be as still as a stone
because of your powerful arm
until your people pass by, Lord,
until the people whom you purchased pass by.

¹⁷ You will bring them in and plant them
on the mountain of your possession;
Lord, you have prepared the place
for your dwelling;
Lord, your hands have established the sanctuary.
¹⁸ The Lord will reign forever and ever!

¹⁹ When Pharaoh's horses with his chariots and horsemen went into the sea, the Lord brought the water of the sea back over them. But the Israelites walked through the sea on dry ground. ²⁰ Then the prophetess Miriam, Aaron's sister, took a tambourine in her hand, and all the women came out following her with tambourines and dancing. ²¹ Miriam sang to them:

Sing to the Lord,
for he is highly exalted;
he has thrown the horse
and its rider into the sea.

Psalm 106:1-12
Israel's Unfaithfulness to God

[1] Hallelujah!
Give thanks to the LORD, for he is good;
his faithful love endures forever.
[2] Who can declare the LORD's mighty acts
or proclaim all the praise due him?
[3] How happy are those who uphold justice,
who practice righteousness at all times.

[4] Remember me, LORD,
when you show favor to your people.
Come to me with your salvation
[5] so that I may enjoy the prosperity
of your chosen ones,
rejoice in the joy of your nation,
and boast about your heritage.

[6] Both we and our fathers have sinned;
we have done wrong and have acted wickedly.
[7] Our fathers in Egypt did not grasp
the significance of your wondrous works
or remember your many acts of faithful love;
instead, they rebelled by the sea—the Red Sea.
[8] Yet he saved them for his name's sake,
to make his power known.
[9] He rebuked the Red Sea, and it dried up;
he led them through the depths as through a desert.
[10] He saved them from the power of the adversary;
he redeemed them from the power of the enemy.
[11] Water covered their foes;
not one of them remained.
[12] Then they believed his promises
and sang his praise.

Romans 6:1-4
The New Life in Christ

[1] What should we say then? Should we continue in sin so that grace may multiply?
[2] Absolutely not! How can we who died to sin still live in it? [3] Or are you unaware that all of us who were baptized into Christ Jesus were baptized into his death? [4] Therefore we were buried with him by baptism into death, in order that, just as Christ was raised from the dead by the glory of the Father, so we too may walk in newness of life.

Month   Day

Notes

Day 12
The Lord Provides in the Wilderness

Exodus 15:22-27
Water Provided

Then Moses led Israel on from the Red Sea, and they went out to the Wilderness of Shur. They journeyed for three days in the wilderness without finding water. ²³ They came to Marah, but they could not drink the water at Marah because it was bitter—that is why it was named Marah. ²⁴ The people grumbled to Moses, "What are we going to drink?" ²⁵ So he cried out to the Lord, and the Lord showed him a tree. When he threw it into the water, the water became drinkable.

The Lord made a statute and ordinance for them at Marah, and he tested them there. ²⁶ He said, "If you will carefully obey the Lord your God, do what is right in his sight, pay attention to his commands, and keep all his statutes, I will not inflict any illnesses on you that I inflicted on the Egyptians. For I am the Lord who heals you."

²⁷ Then they came to Elim, where there were twelve springs and seventy date palms, and they camped there by the water.

Exodus 16
Manna and Quail Provided

¹ The entire Israelite community departed from Elim and came to the Wilderness of Sin, which is between Elim and Sinai, on the fifteenth day of the second month after they had left the land of Egypt. ² The entire Israelite community grumbled against Moses and Aaron in the wilderness. ³ The Israelites said to them, "If only we had died by the Lord's hand in the land of Egypt, when we sat by pots of meat and ate all the bread we wanted. Instead, you brought us into this wilderness to make this whole assembly die of hunger!"

Section 2
For Glory and Beauty

Exodus 18-40

In the second half of Exodus, God teaches His people how to worship Him in the wilderness. For the glory and beauty of His name, God gives Israel His law, plans for building His tabernacle, and instruction for how to set apart His priests for service.

Day 15
Jethro's Visit

Exodus 18
Jethro's Visit

Moses's father-in-law Jethro, the priest of Midian, heard about everything that God had done for Moses and for God's people Israel when the LORD brought Israel out of Egypt.

² Now Jethro, Moses's father-in-law, had taken in Zipporah, Moses's wife, after he had sent her back, ³ along with her two sons, one of whom was named Gershom (because Moses had said, "I have been a resident alien in a foreign land") ⁴ and the other Eliezer (because he had said, "The God of my father was my helper and rescued me from Pharaoh's sword").

⁵ Moses's father-in-law Jethro, along with Moses's wife and sons, came to him in the wilderness where he was camped at the mountain of God. ⁶ He sent word to Moses, "I, your father-in-law Jethro, am coming to you with your wife and her two sons."

⁷ So Moses went out to meet his father-in-law, bowed down, and then kissed him. They asked each other how they had been and went into the tent. ⁸ Moses recounted to his father-in-law all that the LORD had done to Pharaoh and the Egyptians for Israel's sake, all the hardships that confronted them on the way, and how the LORD rescued them.

⁹ Jethro rejoiced over all the good things the LORD had done for Israel when he rescued them from the power of the Egyptians. ¹⁰ "Blessed be the LORD," Jethro exclaimed, "who rescued you from the power of Egypt and from the power of Pharaoh. He has rescued the people from under the power of Egypt! ¹¹ Now I know that the LORD is greater than all gods, because he did wonders when the Egyptians acted arrogantly against Israel."

12 Then Jethro, Moses's father-in-law, brought a burnt offering and sacrifices to God, and Aaron came with all the elders of Israel to eat a meal with Moses's father-in-law in God's presence.

13 The next day Moses sat down to judge the people, and they stood around Moses from morning until evening. 14 When Moses's father-in-law saw everything he was doing for them he asked, "What is this thing you're doing for the people? Why are you alone sitting as judge, while all the people stand around you from morning until evening?"

15 Moses replied to his father-in-law, "Because the people come to me to inquire of God. 16 Whenever they have a dispute, it comes to me, and I make a decision between one man and another. I teach them God's statutes and laws."

17 "What you're doing is not good," Moses's father-in-law said to him. 18 "You will certainly wear out both yourself and these people who are with you, because the task is too heavy for you. You can't do it alone. 19 Now listen to me; I will give you some advice, and God be with you. You be the one to represent the people before God and bring their cases to him. 20 Instruct them about the statutes and laws, and teach them the way to live and what they must do. 21 But you should select from all the people able men, God-fearing, trustworthy, and hating dishonest profit. Place them over the people as commanders of thousands, hundreds, fifties, and tens. 22 They should judge the people at all times. Then they can bring you every major case but judge every minor case themselves. In this way you will lighten your load, and they will bear it with you. 23 If you do this, and God so directs you, you will be able to endure, and also all these people will be able to go home satisfied."

24 Moses listened to his father-in-law and did everything he said. 25 So Moses chose able men from all Israel and made them leaders over the people as commanders of thousands, hundreds, fifties, and tens. 26 They judged the people at all times; they would bring the hard cases to Moses, but they would judge every minor case themselves.

27 Moses let his father-in-law go, and he journeyed to his own land.

Deuteronomy 17:8-11
Difficult Cases

8 If a case is too difficult for you—concerning bloodshed, lawsuits, or assaults—cases disputed at your city gates, then go up to the place the LORD your God chooses. 9 You are to go to the Levitical priests and to the judge who presides at that time. Ask, and they will give you a verdict in the case. 10 You must abide by the verdict they give you at the place the LORD chooses. Be careful to do exactly

"Now I know that the LORD is greater than all gods..." EXODUS 18:11

as they instruct you. [11] You must abide by the instruction they give you and the verdict they announce to you. Do not turn to the right or the left from the decision they declare to you.

Acts 6:1-7
Seven Chosen to Serve

[1] In those days, as the disciples were increasing in number, there arose a complaint by the Hellenistic Jews against the Hebraic Jews that their widows were being overlooked in the daily distribution. [2] The Twelve summoned the whole company of the disciples and said, "It would not be right for us to give up preaching the word of God to wait on tables. [3] Brothers and sisters, select from among you seven men of good reputation, full of the Spirit and wisdom, whom we can appoint to this duty. [4] But we will devote ourselves to prayer and to the ministry of the word." [5] This proposal pleased the whole company. So they chose Stephen, a man full of faith and the Holy Spirit, and Philip, Prochorus, Nicanor, Timon, Parmenas, and Nicolaus, a convert from Antioch. [6] They had them stand before the apostles, who prayed and laid their hands on them.

[7] So the word of God spread,

the disciples in Jerusalem increased greatly in number, and a large group of priests became obedient to the faith.

Notes

Day 16
The Ten Commandments

Exodus 19
Israel at Sinai

In the third month from the very day the Israelites left the land of Egypt, they came to the Sinai Wilderness. ² They traveled from Rephidim, came to the Sinai Wilderness, and camped in the wilderness. Israel camped there in front of the mountain.

³ Moses went up the mountain to God, and the Lord called to him from the mountain: "This is what you must say to the house of Jacob and explain to the Israelites: ⁴ 'You have seen what I did to the Egyptians and how I carried you on eagles' wings and brought you to myself. ⁵ Now if you will carefully listen to me and keep my covenant, you will be my own possession out of all the peoples, although the whole earth is mine, ⁶ and you will be my kingdom of priests and my holy nation.' These are the words that you are to say to the Israelites."

⁷ After Moses came back, he summoned the elders of the people and set before them all these words that the Lord had commanded him. ⁸ Then all the people responded together, "We will do all that the Lord has spoken." So Moses brought the people's words back to the Lord.

⁹ The Lord said to Moses, "I am going to come to you in a dense cloud, so that the people will hear when I speak with you and will always believe you." Moses reported the people's words to the Lord, ¹⁰ and the Lord told Moses, "Go to the people and consecrate them today and tomorrow. They must wash their clothes ¹¹ and be prepared by the third day, for on the third day the Lord will come down on Mount Sinai in the sight of all the people. ¹² Put boundaries for the people all around the mountain and say: Be careful that you don't go up on the mountain or touch its base. Anyone who touches the mountain must be put to death. ¹³ No hand

may touch him; instead he will be stoned or shot with arrows and not live, whether animal or human. When the ram's horn sounds a long blast, they may go up the mountain."

¹⁴ Then Moses came down from the mountain to the people and consecrated them, and they washed their clothes. ¹⁵ He said to the people, "Be prepared by the third day. Do not have sexual relations with women."

¹⁶ On the third day, when morning came, there was thunder and lightning, a thick cloud on the mountain, and a very loud trumpet sound, so that all the people in the camp shuddered. ¹⁷ Then Moses brought the people out of the camp to meet God, and they stood at the foot of the mountain. ¹⁸ Mount Sinai was completely enveloped in smoke because the LORD came down on it in fire. Its smoke went up like the smoke of a furnace, and the whole mountain shook violently. ¹⁹ As the sound of the trumpet grew louder and louder, Moses spoke and God answered him in the thunder.

²⁰ The LORD came down on Mount Sinai at the top of the mountain. Then the LORD summoned Moses to the top of the mountain, and he went up. ²¹ The LORD directed Moses, "Go down and warn the people not to break through to see the LORD; otherwise many of them will die. ²² Even the priests who come near the LORD must consecrate themselves, or the LORD will break out in anger against them."

²³ Moses responded to the LORD, "The people cannot come up Mount Sinai, since you warned us: Put a boundary around the mountain and consecrate it." ²⁴ And the LORD replied to him, "Go down and come back with Aaron. But the priests and the people must not break through to come up to the LORD, or he will break out in anger against them." ²⁵ So Moses went down to the people and told them.

Exodus 20:1-21
The Ten Commandments

¹ Then God spoke all these words:

² I am the LORD your God, who brought you out of the land of Egypt, out of the place of slavery.

³ Do not have other gods besides me.

⁴ Do not make an idol for yourself, whether in the shape of anything in the heavens above or on the earth below or in the waters under the earth. ⁵ Do not bow in worship to them, and do not serve them; for I, the LORD your God, am a jealous God, punishing the children for the fathers' iniquity, to the third and fourth generations of those who hate me, ⁶ but showing faithful love to a thousand generations of those who love me and keep my commands.

Moses spoke and God answered him in the thunder. EXODUS 19:19

7 Do not misuse the name of the LORD your God, because the LORD will not leave anyone unpunished who misuses his name.

8 Remember the Sabbath day, to keep it holy: 9 You are to labor six days and do all your work, 10 but the seventh day is a Sabbath to the LORD your God. You must not do any work—you, your son or daughter, your male or female servant, your livestock, or the resident alien who is within your city gates. 11 For the LORD made the heavens and the earth, the sea, and everything in them in six days; then he rested on the seventh day. Therefore the LORD blessed the Sabbath day and declared it holy.

12 Honor your father and your mother so that you may have a long life in the land that the LORD your God is giving you.

13 Do not murder.

14 Do not commit adultery.

15 Do not steal.

16 Do not give false testimony against your neighbor.

17 Do not covet your neighbor's house. Do not covet your neighbor's wife, his male or female servant, his ox or donkey, or anything that belongs to your neighbor.

The People's Reaction

18 All the people witnessed the thunder and lightning, the sound of the trumpet, and the mountain surrounded by smoke. When the people saw it they trembled and stood at a distance. 19 "You speak to us, and we will listen," they said to Moses, "but don't let God speak to us, or we will die."

20 Moses responded to the people, "Don't be afraid, for God has come to test you, so that you will fear him and will not sin." 21 And the people remained standing at a distance as Moses approached the total darkness where God was.

John 1:14-17

14 The Word became flesh and dwelt among us. We observed his glory, the glory as the one and only Son from the Father, full of grace and truth. 15 (John testified concerning him and exclaimed, "This was the one of whom I said, 'The one coming after me ranks ahead of me, because he existed before me.'") 16 Indeed, we have all received grace upon grace from his fullness, 17 for the law was given through Moses; grace and truth came through Jesus Christ.

Hebrews 8:7-13

A Superior Covenant

[7] For if that first covenant had been faultless, there would have been no occasion
for a second one. [8] But finding fault with his people, he says:

See, the days are coming, says the Lord,
when I will make a new covenant
with the house of Israel
and with the house of Judah—
[9] not like the covenant
that I made with their ancestors
on the day I took them by the hand
to lead them out of the land of Egypt.
I showed no concern for them, says the Lord,
because they did not continue in my covenant.
[10] For this is the covenant
that I will make with the house of Israel
after those days, says the Lord:

I will put my laws into their minds
and write them on their hearts.

I will be their God,
and they will be my people.
[11] And each person will not teach his fellow citizen,
and each his brother or sister, saying, "Know the Lord,"
because they will all know me,
from the least to the greatest of them.
[12] For I will forgive their wrongdoing,
and I will never again remember their sins.

[13] By saying a new covenant, he has declared that the first is obsolete. And what
is obsolete and growing old is about to pass away.

NOTES

Day 17
Moses Receives
Additional Laws

Exodus 20:22-26
Moses Receives Additional Laws

Then the Lord told Moses, "This is what you are to say to the Israelites: You have seen that I have spoken to you from heaven. ²³ Do not make gods of silver to rival me; do not make gods of gold for yourselves.

²⁴ "Make an earthen altar for me, and sacrifice on it your burnt offerings and fellowship offerings, your flocks and herds. I will come to you and bless you in every place where I cause my name to be remembered. ²⁵ If you make a stone altar for me, do not build it out of cut stones. If you use your chisel on it, you will defile it. ²⁶ Do not go up to my altar on steps, so that your nakedness is not exposed on it."

Exodus 21

¹ "These are the ordinances that you are to set before them:

Laws About Slaves

² "When you buy a Hebrew slave, he is to serve for six years; then in the seventh he is to leave as a free man without paying anything. ³ If he arrives alone, he is to leave alone; if he arrives with a wife, his wife is to leave with him. ⁴ If his master gives him a wife and she bears him sons or daughters, the wife and her children belong to her master, and the man must leave alone.

⁵ "But if the slave declares, 'I love my master, my wife, and my children; I do not want to leave as a free man,' ⁶ his master is to bring him to the judges and then bring him to the door or doorpost. His master will pierce his ear with an awl, and he will serve his master for life.

7 "When a man sells his daughter as a concubine, she is not to leave as the male slaves do. 8 If she is displeasing to her master, who chose her for himself, then he must let her be redeemed. He has no right to sell her to foreigners because he has acted treacherously toward her. 9 Or if he chooses her for his son, he must deal with her according to the customary treatment of daughters. 10 If he takes an additional wife, he must not reduce the food, clothing, or marital rights of the first wife. 11 And if he does not do these three things for her, she may leave free of charge, without any payment.

Laws About Personal Injury

12 "Whoever strikes a person so that he dies must be put to death. 13 But if he did not intend any harm, and yet God allowed it to happen, I will appoint a place for you where he may flee. 14 If a person schemes and willfully acts against his neighbor to murder him, you must take him from my altar to be put to death.

15 "Whoever strikes his father or his mother must be put to death.

16 "Whoever kidnaps a person must be put to death, whether he sells him or the person is found in his possession.

17 "Whoever curses his father or his mother must be put to death.

18 "When men quarrel and one strikes the other with a stone or his fist, and the injured man does not die but is confined to bed, 19 if he can later get up and walk around outside leaning on his staff, then the one who struck him will be exempt from punishment. Nevertheless, he must pay for his lost work time and provide for his complete recovery.

20 "When a man strikes his male or female slave with a rod, and the slave dies under his abuse, the owner must be punished. 21 However, if the slave can stand up after a day or two, the owner should not be punished because he is his owner's property.

22 "When men get in a fight and hit a pregnant woman so that her children are born prematurely but there is no injury, the one who hit her must be fined as the woman's husband demands from him, and he must pay according to judicial assessment. 23 If there is an injury, then you must give life for life, 24 eye for eye, tooth for tooth, hand for hand, foot for foot, 25 burn for burn, bruise for bruise, wound for wound.

26 "When a man strikes the eye of his male or female slave and destroys it, he must let the slave go free in compensation for his eye. 27 If he knocks out the tooth of his male or female slave, he must let the slave go free in compensation for his tooth.

28 "When an ox gores a man or a woman to death, the ox must be stoned, and its meat may not be eaten, but the ox's owner is innocent. 29 However, if the ox

"I will come to you and bless you in every place where I cause my name to be remembered." EXODUS 20:24

was in the habit of goring, and its owner has been warned yet does not restrain it, and it kills a man or a woman, the ox must be stoned, and its owner must also be put to death. [30] If instead a ransom is demanded of him, he can pay a redemption price for his life in the full amount demanded from him. [31] If it gores a son or a daughter, he is to be dealt with according to this same law. [32] If the ox gores a male or female slave, he must give thirty shekels of silver to the slave's master, and the ox must be stoned.

[33] "When a man uncovers a pit or digs a pit, and does not cover it, and an ox or a donkey falls into it, [34] the owner of the pit must give compensation; he must pay to its owner, but the dead animal will become his.

[35] "When a man's ox injures his neighbor's ox and it dies, they must sell the live ox and divide its proceeds; they must also divide the dead animal. [36] If, however, it is known that the ox was in the habit of goring, yet its owner has not restrained it, he must compensate fully, ox for ox; the dead animal will become his."

Isaiah 44:6

This is what the LORD, the King of Israel and its Redeemer, the LORD of Armies, says:

> I am the first and I am the last.
> There is no God but me.

Matthew 22:36-40

[36] "Teacher, which command in the law is the greatest?"

[37] He said to him,

"Love the Lord your God with all your heart, with all your soul, and with all your mind.

[38] This is the greatest and most important command. [39] The second is like it: Love your neighbor as yourself. [40] All the Law and the Prophets depend on these two commands."

Notes

Day 18
Honesty and Justice

Exodus 22
Laws About Theft

When a man steals an ox or a sheep and butchers it or sells it, he must repay five cattle for the ox or four sheep for the sheep. [2] If a thief is caught in the act of breaking in, and he is beaten to death, no one is guilty of bloodshed. [3] But if this happens after sunrise, the householder is guilty of bloodshed. A thief must make full restitution. If he is unable, he is to be sold because of his theft. [4] If what was stolen—whether ox, donkey, or sheep—is actually found alive in his possession, he must repay double.

Laws About Crop Protection

[5] "When a man lets a field or vineyard be grazed in, and then allows his animals to go and graze in someone else's field, he must repay with the best of his own field or vineyard.

[6] "When a fire gets out of control, spreads to thornbushes, and consumes stacks of cut grain, standing grain, or a field, the one who started the fire must make full restitution for what was burned.

Laws About Personal Property

[7] "When a man gives his neighbor valuables or goods to keep, but they are stolen from that person's house, the thief, if caught, must repay double. [8] If the thief is not caught, the owner of the house must present himself to the judges to determine whether or not he has taken his neighbor's property. [9] In any case of wrongdoing involving an ox, a donkey, a sheep, a garment, or anything else lost, and someone claims, 'That's mine,' the case between the two parties is to come before the judges. The one the judges condemn must repay double to his neighbor.

[10] "When a man gives his neighbor a donkey, an ox, a sheep, or any other animal to care for, but it dies, is injured, or is stolen, while no one is watching, [11] there must be an oath before the LORD between the two of them to determine whether or not he has taken his neighbor's property. Its owner must accept the oath, and the other man does not have to make restitution. [12] But if, in fact, the animal was stolen from his custody, he must make restitution to its owner. [13] If it was actually torn apart by a wild animal, he is to bring it as evidence; he does not have to make restitution for the torn carcass.

[14] "When a man borrows an animal from his neighbor, and it is injured or dies while its owner is not there with it, the man must make full restitution. [15] If its owner is there with it, the man does not have to make restitution. If it was rented, the loss is covered by its rental price.

Laws About Seduction

[16] "If a man seduces a virgin who is not engaged, and he sleeps with her, he must certainly pay the bridal price for her to be his wife. [17] If her father absolutely refuses to give her to him, he must pay an amount in silver equal to the bridal price for virgins.

Capital Offenses

[18] "Do not allow a sorceress to live.

[19] "Whoever has sexual intercourse with an animal must be put to death.

[20] "Whoever sacrifices to any gods, except the LORD alone, is to be set apart for destruction.

Laws Protecting the Vulnerable

[21] "You must not exploit a resident alien or oppress him, since you were resident aliens in the land of Egypt.

[22] "You must not mistreat any widow or fatherless child. [23] If you do mistreat them, they will no doubt cry to me, and I will certainly hear their cry. [24] My anger will burn, and I will kill you with the sword; then your wives will be widows and your children fatherless.

[25] "If you lend silver to my people, to the poor person among you, you must not be like a creditor to him; you must not charge him interest.

[26] "If you ever take your neighbor's cloak as collateral, return it to him before sunset. [27] For it is his only covering; it is the clothing for his body. What will he sleep in? And if he cries out to me, I will listen because I am gracious.

"Be my holy people." EXODUS 22:31

Respect for God

²⁸ "You must not blaspheme God or curse a leader among your people.

²⁹ "You must not hold back offerings from your harvest or your vats. Give me the firstborn of your sons. ³⁰ Do the same with your cattle and your flock. Let them stay with their mothers for seven days, but on the eighth day you are to give them to me.

³¹ "Be my holy people. You must not eat the meat of a mauled animal found in the field; throw it to the dogs."

Exodus 23:1-19
Laws About Honesty and Justice

¹ "You must not spread a false report. Do not join the wicked to be a malicious witness.

² "You must not follow a crowd in wrongdoing. Do not testify in a lawsuit and go along with a crowd to pervert justice. ³ Do not show favoritism to a poor person in his lawsuit.

⁴ "If you come across your enemy's stray ox or donkey, you must return it to him.

⁵ "If you see the donkey of someone who hates you lying helpless under its load, and you want to refrain from helping it, you must help with it.

⁶ "You must not deny justice to a poor person among you in his lawsuit. ⁷ Stay far away from a false accusation. Do not kill the innocent and the just, because I will not justify the guilty. ⁸ You must not take a bribe, for a bribe blinds the clear-sighted and corrupts the words of the righteous. ⁹ You must not oppress a resident alien; you yourselves know how it feels to be a resident alien because you were resident aliens in the land of Egypt.

Sabbaths and Festivals

¹⁰ "Sow your land for six years and gather its produce. ¹¹ But during the seventh year you are to let it rest and leave it uncultivated, so that the poor among your people may eat from it and the wild animals may consume what they leave. Do the same with your vineyard and your olive grove.

¹² "Do your work for six days but rest on the seventh day so that your ox and your donkey may rest, and the son of your female slave as well as the resident alien may be refreshed.

¹³ "Pay strict attention to everything I have said to you. You must not invoke the names of other gods; they must not be heard on your lips.

¹⁴ "Celebrate a festival in my honor three times a year. ¹⁵ Observe the Festival of Unleavened Bread. As I commanded you, you are to eat unleavened bread for seven days at the appointed time in the month of Abib, because you came out of Egypt in that month. No one is to appear before me empty-handed. ¹⁶ Also observe the Festival of Harvest with the firstfruits of your produce from what you sow in the field, and observe the Festival of Ingathering at the end of the year, when you gather your produce from the field. ¹⁷ Three times a year all your males are to appear before the Lord GOD.

¹⁸ "You must not offer the blood of my sacrifices with anything leavened. The fat of my festival offering must not remain until morning.

¹⁹ "Bring the best of the firstfruits of your land to the house of the LORD your God.

"You must not boil a young goat in its mother's milk."

Proverbs 31:8-9

⁸ Speak up for those who have no voice,
for the justice of all who are dispossessed.
⁹ Speak up, judge righteously,
and defend the cause of the oppressed and needy.

1 Corinthians 10:24

No one is to seek his own good, but the good of the other person.

The Life of Moses

Moses Flees

Moses kills Egyptian
guard and retreats to the
land of Midian where he
marries Zipporah.

EXODUS 2:11-22

Banks of the Nile

AGE 40

3 MONTHS OLD

Midian

**Pharaoh Threatens
Hebrew Sons**

Pharaoh's daughter finds
baby Moses in the Nile.

EXODUS 2:1-10

Mount Horeb

Burning Bush

Moses encounters God and is sent to deliver Israel from slavery in Egypt.

EXODUS 3

Egypt

Moses Returns to Egypt

Moses and Aaron appeal to Pharaoh to let Israel go. Pharaoh refuses and forces the enslaved Israelites to make bricks without straw.

EXODUS 4-6

Ten Plagues

Pharaoh refuses to let Israel go. God sends ten plagues against Egypt.

EXODUS 7:1-12:30

The Red Sea

The Exodus and Crossing the Red Sea

After the tenth plague, the death of the firstborn sons, Pharaoh tells Israel to leave. Moses leads Israel from the Egyptian wilderness through the Red Sea.

EXODUS 12:31-15:21

Western Sinai Peninsula

Wilderness Wandering

God sends manna and quail, provides water from a rock.

EXODUS 16:22-17:7

Mount Sinai

Ten Commandments

God delivers His law to Moses and gives Moses two stone tablets bearing the Ten Commandments.

EXODUS 20:1-17

Aaron and Israel Make a Gold Calf

When Moses sees it, he throws down the stone tablets bearing the Ten Commandments.

EXODUS 32

Covenant Renewal

Moses intercedes on behalf of the Israelites, and God renews His covenant with Israel. Moses' face is radiant after speaking with God.

EXODUS 33-34

AGE 80-81

AGE 81-120

AGE 120

Eastern Sinai Peninsula

Wilderness Wanderings

When the Israelites refuse to enter the Promised Land, God has the entire nation wander in the wilderness for forty years until the last of that generation dies.

NUMBERS 14:20-35

Moab

Joshua Appointed

Moses names Joshua as his successor, the leader who will take the Israelites into the Promised Land after forty years in the wilderness, Edom, and Moab.

DEUTERONOMY 31:1-8

Mount Nebo

Moses Dies

God takes Moses up to Mount Nebo so he can look over the Promised Land that Joshua is about to enter with Israel. Moses dies, and God buries him in a secret place.

DEUTERONOMY 34

Day 19
The Covenant Ceremony

Exodus 23:20-33
Promises and Warnings

I am going to send an angel before you to protect you on the way and bring you to the place I have prepared. [21] Be attentive to him and listen to him. Do not defy him, because he will not forgive your acts of rebellion, for my name is in him. [22] But if you will carefully obey him and do everything I say, then I will be an enemy to your enemies and a foe to your foes. [23] For my angel will go before you and bring you to the land of the Amorites, Hethites, Perizzites, Canaanites, Hivites, and Jebusites, and I will wipe them out. [24] Do not bow in worship to their gods, and do not serve them. Do not imitate their practices. Instead, demolish them and smash their sacred pillars to pieces. [25] Serve the LORD your God, and he will bless your bread and your water. I will remove illnesses from you. [26] No woman will miscarry or be childless in your land. I will give you the full number of your days.

[27] "I will cause the people ahead of you to feel terror and will throw into confusion all the nations you come to. I will make all your enemies turn their backs to you in retreat. [28] I will send hornets in front of you, and they will drive the Hivites, Canaanites, and Hethites away from you. [29] I will not drive them out ahead of you in a single year; otherwise, the land would become desolate, and wild animals would multiply against you. [30] I will drive them out little by little ahead of you until you have become numerous and take possession of the land. [31] I will set your borders from the Red Sea to the Mediterranean Sea, and from the wilderness to the Euphrates River. For I will place the inhabitants of the land under your control, and you will drive them out ahead of you. [32] You must not make a covenant with them or their gods. [33] They must not remain in your land, or else they will make you sin against me. If you serve their gods, it will be a snare for you."

Exodus 24
The Covenant Ceremony

[1] Then he said to Moses, "Go up to the LORD, you and Aaron, Nadab, and Abihu, and seventy of Israel's elders, and bow in worship at a distance. [2] Moses alone is to approach the LORD, but the others are not to approach, and the people are not to go up with him."

[3] Moses came and told the people all the commands of the LORD and all the ordinances. Then all the people responded with a single voice, "We will do everything that the LORD has commanded." [4] And Moses wrote down all the words of the LORD. He rose early the next morning and set up an altar and twelve pillars for the twelve tribes of Israel at the base of the mountain. [5] Then he sent out young Israelite men, and they offered burnt offerings and sacrificed bulls as fellowship offerings to the LORD. [6] Moses took half the blood and set it in basins; the other half of the blood he splattered on the altar. [7] He then took the covenant scroll and read it aloud to the people. They responded, "We will do and obey all that the LORD has commanded."

[8] Moses took the blood, splattered it on the people, and said, "This is the blood of the covenant that the LORD has made with you concerning all these words."

[9] Then Moses went up with Aaron, Nadab, and Abihu, and seventy of Israel's elders, [10] and they saw the God of Israel. Beneath his feet was something like a pavement made of lapis lazuli, as clear as the sky itself. [11] God did not harm the Israelite nobles; they saw him, and they ate and drank.

[12] The LORD said to Moses, "Come up to me on the mountain and stay there so that I may give you the stone tablets with the law and commandments I have written for their instruction."

[13] So Moses arose with his assistant Joshua and went up the mountain of God. [14] He told the elders, "Wait here for us until we return to you. Aaron and Hur are here with you. Whoever has a dispute should go to them." [15] When Moses went up the mountain, the cloud covered it. [16] The glory of the LORD settled on Mount Sinai, and the cloud covered it for six days. On the seventh day he called to Moses from the cloud. [17] The appearance of the LORD's glory to the Israelites was like a consuming fire on the mountaintop. [18] Moses entered the cloud as he went up the mountain, and he remained on the mountain forty days and forty nights.

Exodus 25
Offerings to Build the Tabernacle

[1] The LORD spoke to Moses: [2] "Tell the Israelites to take an offering for me. You are to take my offering from everyone who is willing to give. [3] This is the offering you are to receive from them: gold, silver, and bronze; [4] blue, purple, and scarlet yarn; fine linen and goat hair; [5] ram skins dyed red and fine leather; acacia wood; [6] oil for the light; spices for the anointing oil and for the fragrant incense; [7] and onyx along with other gemstones for mounting on the ephod and breastpiece.

[8] "They are to make a sanctuary for me so that I may dwell among them. [9] You must make it according to all that I show you—the pattern of the tabernacle as well as the pattern of all its furnishings.

The Ark

[10] "They are to make an ark of acacia wood, forty-five inches long, twenty-seven inches wide, and twenty-seven inches high. [11] Overlay it with pure gold; overlay it both inside and out. Also make a gold molding all around it. [12] Cast four gold rings for it and place them on its four feet, two rings on one side and two rings on the other side. [13] Make poles of acacia wood and overlay them with gold. [14] Insert the poles into the rings on the sides of the ark in order to carry the ark with them. [15] The poles

"We will do and obey all that the LORD has commanded." EXODUS 24:7

are to remain in the rings of the ark; they must not be removed from it. ¹⁶ Put the tablets of the testimony that I will give you into the ark. ¹⁷ Make a mercy seat of pure gold, forty-five inches long and twenty-seven inches wide. ¹⁸ Make two cherubim of gold; make them of hammered work at the two ends of the mercy seat. ¹⁹ Make one cherub at one end and one cherub at the other end. At its two ends, make the cherubim of one piece with the mercy seat. ²⁰ The cherubim are to have wings spread out above, covering the mercy seat with their wings, and are to face one another. The faces of the cherubim should be toward the mercy seat. ²¹ Set the mercy seat on top of the ark and put the tablets of the testimony that I will give you into the ark. ²² I will meet with you there above the mercy seat, between the two cherubim that are over the ark of the testimony; I will speak with you from there about all that I command you regarding the Israelites.

The Table

²³ "You are to construct a table of acacia wood, thirty-six inches long, eighteen inches wide, and twenty-seven inches high. ²⁴ Overlay it with pure gold and make a gold molding all around it. ²⁵ Make a three-inch frame all around it and make a gold molding for it all around its frame. ²⁶ Make four gold rings for it, and attach the rings to the four corners at its four legs. ²⁷ The rings should be next to the frame as holders for the poles to carry the table. ²⁸ Make the poles of acacia wood and overlay them with gold, and the table can be carried by them. ²⁹ You are also to make its plates and cups, as well as its pitchers and bowls for pouring drink offerings. Make them out of pure gold. ³⁰ Put the Bread of the Presence on the table before me at all times.

The Lampstand

³¹ "You are to make a lampstand out of pure, hammered gold. It is to be made of one piece: its base and shaft, its ornamental cups, and its buds and petals. ³² Six branches are to extend from its sides, three branches of the lampstand from one side and three branches of the lampstand from the other side. ³³ There are to be three cups shaped like almond blossoms, each with a bud and petals, on one branch, and three cups shaped like almond blossoms, each with a bud and petals, on the next branch. It is to be this way for the six branches that extend from the lampstand. ³⁴ There are to be four cups shaped like almond blossoms on the lampstand shaft along with its buds and petals. ³⁵ For the six branches that extend from the lampstand, a bud must be under the first pair of branches from it, a bud under the second pair of branches from it, and a bud under the third pair of branches from it. ³⁶ Their buds and branches are to be of one piece. All of it is to be a single hammered piece of pure gold.

³⁷ "Make its seven lamps, and set them up so that they illuminate the area in front of it. ³⁸ Its snuffers and firepans must be of pure gold. ³⁹ The lampstand with all these utensils is to be made from seventy-five pounds of pure gold. ⁴⁰ Be careful to make them according to the pattern you have been shown on the mountain."

Matthew 26:26-29
The First Lord's Supper

²⁶ As they were eating, Jesus took bread, blessed and broke it, gave it to the disciples, and said, "Take and eat it; this is my body." ²⁷ Then he took a cup, and after giving thanks, he gave it to them and said, "Drink from it, all of you. ²⁸ For this is my blood of the covenant, which is poured out for many for the forgiveness of sins. ²⁹ But I tell you, I will not drink from this fruit of the vine from now on until that day when I drink it new with you in my Father's kingdom."

Hebrews 9:18-22

¹⁸ That is why even the first covenant was inaugurated with blood. ¹⁹ For when every command had been proclaimed by Moses to all the people according to the law, he took the blood of calves and goats, along with water, scarlet wool, and hyssop, and sprinkled the scroll itself and all the people, ²⁰ saying,

This is the blood of the covenant that God has ordained for you.

²¹ In the same way, he sprinkled the tabernacle and all the articles of worship with blood. ²² According to the law almost everything is purified with blood, and without the shedding of blood there is no forgiveness.

Day 20
Grace Day

Use today to pray, rest, and reflect on this week's reading, giving thanks for the grace that is ours in Christ.

For this is the covenant
that I will make with the house of Israel
after those days, says the Lord:
I will put my laws into their minds
and write them on their hearts.
I will be their God,
and they will be my people.

HEBREWS 8:10

Black Pepper Salmon and Zucchini Noodle Bowl

TOTAL TIME: 30 MINUTES

SERVES: 1

INGREDIENTS

8 ounces salmon

Salt and pepper

Olive oil

1 tablespoon garlic

½ small red onion

1 14-ounce can lite coconut milk

1 tablespoon curry powder

⅛ teaspoon cinnamon

1 14.5-ounce can stewed tomatoes

1 tablespoon fresh thyme

1 small zucchini

5 basil leaves

DIRECTIONS

Preheat oven to 350°F.

Line baking sheet with parchment paper. Place salmon on sheet and sprinkle liberally with salt and pepper. Bake 15-20 minutes.

Heat olive oil in a saucepan over medium heat. Add garlic and red onion and cook until onion starts to soften, about 5 minutes. Add coconut milk, curry powder, cinnamon, and a sprinkle of salt. Stir for several minutes. Add stewed tomatoes and thyme. Let simmer.

To create zucchini noodles, use a vegetable peeler to cut lengthwise into wide slices, stopping when the seeds are reached. Turn zucchini over and continue peeling until all the zucchini is in long strips. Discard seeds. Slice the zucchini into thinner strips resembling linguini and add to the sauce.

Transfer the sauce and noodles into a bowl. Place the salmon in the broth and garnish with fresh basil.

Day 21
Weekly Truth

"I am the LORD your God, who brought you out of the land of Egypt, out of the place of slavery."

EXODUS 20:2

Scripture is God-breathed and true. When we memorize it, we carry the gospel with us wherever we go.

This week's verse is the key verse for the book of Exodus.

Find the corresponding memory card in the back of your book.

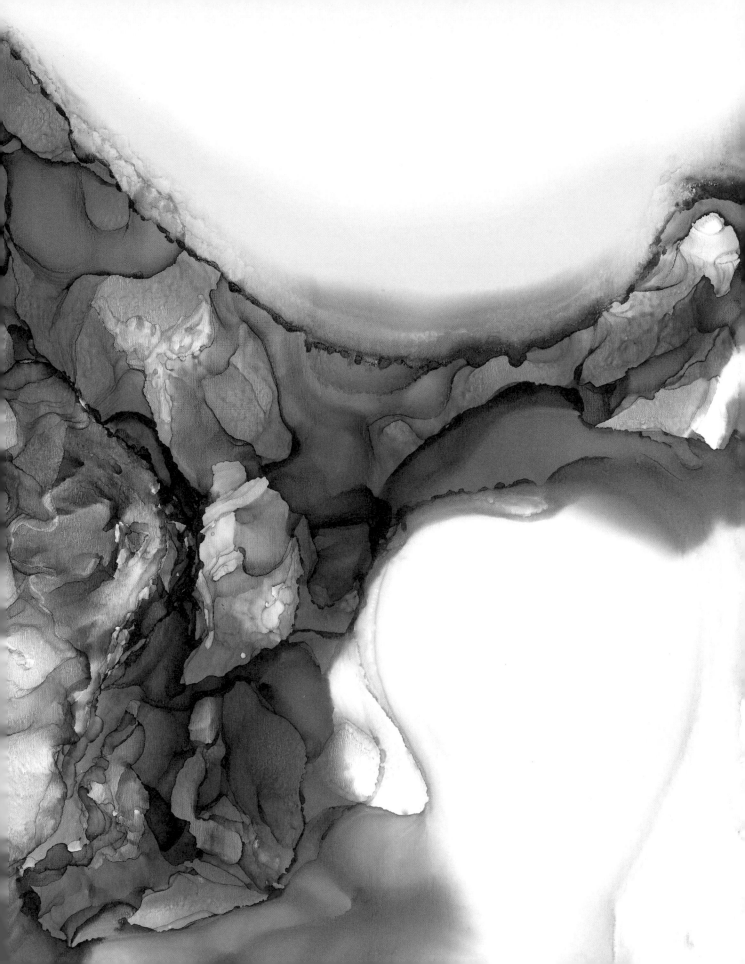

Day 22
Instructions for the Tabernacle

Exodus 26
The Tabernacle

You are to construct the tabernacle itself with ten curtains. You must make them of finely spun linen, and blue, purple, and scarlet yarn, with a design of cherubim worked into them. ² Each curtain should be forty-two feet long and six feet wide; all the curtains are to have the same measurements. ³ Five of the curtains should be joined together, and the other five curtains joined together. ⁴ Make loops of blue yarn on the edge of the last curtain in the first set, and do the same on the edge of the outermost curtain in the second set. ⁵ Make fifty loops on the one curtain and make fifty loops on the edge of the curtain in the second set, so that the loops line up together. ⁶ Also make fifty gold clasps and join the curtains together with the clasps, so that the tabernacle may be a single unit.

⁷ "You are to make curtains of goat hair for a tent over the tabernacle; make eleven of these curtains. ⁸ Each curtain should be forty-five feet long and six feet wide. All eleven curtains are to have the same measurements. ⁹ Join five of the curtains by themselves, and the other six curtains by themselves. Then fold the sixth curtain double at the front of the tent. ¹⁰ Make fifty loops on the edge of one curtain, the outermost in the first set, and make fifty loops on the edge of the corresponding curtain of the second set. ¹¹ Make fifty bronze clasps; put the clasps through the loops and join the tent together so that it is a single unit. ¹² As for the flap that remains from the tent curtains, the leftover half curtain is to hang over the back of the tabernacle. ¹³ What remains along the length of the tent curtains—a half yard on one side and a half yard on the other side—should hang over the sides of the tabernacle on either side to cover it. ¹⁴ Make a covering for the tent from ram skins dyed red and a covering of fine leather on top of that.

¹⁵ "You are to make upright supports of acacia wood for the tabernacle. ¹⁶ Each support is to be fifteen feet long and twenty-seven inches wide. ¹⁷ Each support will have two tenons for joining. Do the same for all the supports of the tabernacle. ¹⁸ Make the supports for the tabernacle as follows: twenty supports for the south side, ¹⁹ and make forty silver bases under the twenty supports, two bases under the first support for its two tenons, and two bases under the next support for its two tenons; ²⁰ twenty supports for the second side of the tabernacle, the north side, ²¹ along with their forty silver bases, two bases under the first support and two bases under each support; ²² and make six supports for the west side of the tabernacle. ²³ Make two additional supports for the two back corners of the tabernacle. ²⁴ They are to be paired at the bottom, and joined together at the top in a single ring. So it should be for both of them; they will serve as the two corners. ²⁵ There are to be eight supports with their silver bases: sixteen bases; two bases under the first support and two bases under each support.

²⁶ "You are to make five crossbars of acacia wood for the supports on one side of the tabernacle, ²⁷ five crossbars for the supports on the other side of the tabernacle, and five crossbars for the supports of the back side of the tabernacle on the west. ²⁸ The central crossbar is to run through the middle of the supports from one end to the other. ²⁹ Then overlay the supports with gold, and make their rings of gold as the holders for the crossbars. Also overlay the crossbars with gold. ³⁰ You are to set up the tabernacle according to the plan for it that you have been shown on the mountain.

³¹ "You are to make a curtain of blue, purple, and scarlet yarn, and finely spun linen with a design of cherubim worked into it.

³² Hang it on four gold-plated pillars of acacia wood that have gold hooks and that stand on four silver bases. ³³ Hang the curtain under the clasps and bring the ark of the testimony there behind the curtain, so the curtain will make a separation for you between the holy place and the most holy place. ³⁴ Put the mercy seat on the ark of the testimony in the most holy place. ³⁵ Place the table outside the curtain and the lampstand on the south side of the tabernacle, opposite the table; put the table on the north side.

³⁶ "For the entrance to the tent you are to make a screen embroidered with blue, purple, and scarlet yarn, and finely spun linen. ³⁷ Make five pillars of acacia wood for the screen and overlay them with gold; their hooks are to be gold, and you are to cast five bronze bases for them."

"You are to set up the tabernacle according to the plan for it that you have been shown on the mountain." EXODUS 26:30

Genesis 3:24

He drove the man out and stationed the cherubim and the flaming, whirling sword east of the garden of Eden to guard the way to the tree of life.

Hebrews 9:6-14

[6] With these things prepared like this, the priests enter the first room repeatedly, performing their ministry. [7] But the high priest alone enters the second room, and he does that only once a year, and never without blood, which he offers for himself and for the sins the people had committed in ignorance. [8] The Holy Spirit was making it clear that the way into the most holy place had not yet been disclosed while the first tabernacle was still standing. [9] This is a symbol for the present time, during which gifts and sacrifices are offered that cannot perfect the worshiper's conscience. [10] They are physical regulations and only deal with food, drink, and various washings imposed until the time of the new order.

New Covenant Ministry

[11] But Christ has appeared as a high priest of the good things that have come. In the greater and more perfect tabernacle not made with hands (that is, not of this creation), [12] he entered the most holy place once for all time, not by the blood of goats and calves, but by his own blood, having obtained eternal redemption. [13] For if the blood of goats and bulls and the ashes of a young cow, sprinkling those who are defiled, sanctify for the purification of the flesh, [14] how much more will the blood of Christ, who through the eternal Spirit offered himself without blemish to God, cleanse our consciences from dead works so that we can serve the living God?

Month   Day

Notes

Day 23
The Lampstand Oil

Exodus 27
The Altar of Burnt Offering

Y ou are to construct the altar of acacia wood. The altar must be square, 7½ feet long, and 7½ feet wide; it must be 4½ feet high. ² Make horns for it on its four corners; the horns are to be of one piece. Overlay it with bronze. ³ Make its pots for removing ashes, and its shovels, basins, meat forks, and firepans; make all its utensils of bronze. ⁴ Construct a grate for it of bronze mesh, and make four bronze rings on the mesh at its four corners. ⁵ Set it below, under the altar's ledge, so that the mesh comes halfway up the altar. ⁶ Then make poles for the altar, poles of acacia wood, and overlay them with bronze. ⁷ The poles are to be inserted into the rings so that the poles are on two sides of the altar when it is carried. ⁸ Construct the altar with boards so that it is hollow. They are to make it just as it was shown to you on the mountain.

The Courtyard

⁹ "You are to make the courtyard for the tabernacle. Make hangings for the south side of the courtyard out of finely spun linen, 150 feet long on that side ¹⁰ including twenty posts and twenty bronze bases, with silver hooks and silver bands for the posts. ¹¹ And so make hangings 150 feet long for the north side, including twenty posts and their twenty bronze bases, with silver hooks and silver bands for the posts. ¹² For the width of the courtyard, make hangings 75 feet long for the west side, including their ten posts and their ten bases. ¹³ And for the width of the courtyard on the east side toward the sunrise, 75 feet, ¹⁴ make hangings 22½ feet long for one side of the gate, including their three posts and their three bases. ¹⁵ And make hangings 22½ feet long for the other side, including their three posts and their three bases. ¹⁶ The gate of the courtyard is to have a 30-foot screen embroidered with blue, purple, and scarlet yarn, and finely spun linen. It is to have four posts and their four bases.

¹⁷ "All the posts around the courtyard are to be banded with silver and have silver hooks and bronze bases. ¹⁸ The courtyard is to be 150 feet long, 75 feet wide at each end, and 7½ feet high, all of it made of finely spun linen. The bases of the posts are to be bronze. ¹⁹ All the utensils of the tabernacle for every use and all its tent pegs as well as all the tent pegs of the courtyard are to be made of bronze.

The Lampstand Oil

²⁰ "You are to command the Israelites to bring you pure oil from crushed olives for the light, in order to keep the lamp burning regularly. ²¹ In the tent of meeting outside the curtain that is in front of the testimony, Aaron and his sons are to tend the lamp from evening until morning before the Lord. This is to be a permanent statute for the Israelites throughout their generations."

Zechariah 4
Fifth Vision: Gold Lampstand

¹ The angel who was speaking with me then returned and roused me as one awakened out of sleep. ² He asked me, "What do you see?"

I replied, "I see a solid gold lampstand with a bowl at the top. The lampstand also has seven lamps at the top with seven spouts for each of the lamps. ³ There are also two olive trees beside it, one on the right of the bowl and the other on its left."

⁴ Then I asked the angel who was speaking with me, "What are these, my lord?"

⁵ "Don't you know what they are?" replied the angel who was speaking with me.

I said, "No, my lord."

⁶ So he answered me, "This is the word of the Lord to Zerubbabel:

'Not by strength or by might, but by my Spirit,' says the Lord of Armies.

⁷ 'What are you, great mountain? Before Zerubbabel you will become a plain. And he will bring out the capstone accompanied by shouts of: Grace, grace to it!'"

⁸ Then the word of the Lord came to me: ⁹ "Zerubbabel's hands have laid the foundation of this house, and his hands will complete it. Then you will know that the Lord of Armies has sent me to you. ¹⁰ For who despises the day of small things? These seven eyes of the Lord, which scan throughout the whole earth, will rejoice when they see the ceremonial stone in Zerubbabel's hand."

"Aaron and his sons are to tend the lamp from evening until morning before the Lord." EXODUS 27:21

[11] I asked him, "What are the two olive trees on the right and left of the lampstand?" [12] And I questioned him further, "What are the two streams of the olive trees, from which the golden oil is pouring through the two golden conduits?"

[13] Then he inquired of me, "Don't you know what these are?"

"No, my lord," I replied.

[14] "These are the two anointed ones," he said, "who stand by the Lord of the whole earth."

Revelation 11:1-4
The Two Witnesses

[1] Then I was given a measuring reed like a rod, with these words: "Go and measure the temple of God and the altar, and count those who worship there. [2] But exclude the courtyard outside the temple. Don't measure it, because it is given to the nations, and they will trample the holy city for forty-two months. [3] I will grant my two witnesses authority to prophesy for 1,260 days, dressed in sackcloth." [4] These are the two olive trees and the two lampstands that stand before the Lord of the earth."

Month   Day

Notes

Day 24
Instructions for the Priestly Garments

Exodus 28
The Priestly Garments

Have your brother Aaron, with his sons, come to you from the Israelites to serve me as priest—Aaron, his sons Nadab and Abihu, Eleazar and Ithamar. ² Make holy garments for your brother Aaron, for glory and beauty. ³ You are to instruct all the skilled artisans, whom I have filled with a spirit of wisdom, to make Aaron's garments for consecrating him to serve me as priest. ⁴ These are the garments that they must make: a breastpiece, an ephod, a robe, a specially woven tunic, a turban, and a sash. They are to make holy garments for your brother Aaron and his sons so that they may serve me as priests. ⁵ They should use gold; blue, purple, and scarlet yarn; and fine linen.

The Ephod

⁶ "They are to make the ephod of finely spun linen embroidered with gold, and with blue, purple, and scarlet yarn. ⁷ It must have two shoulder pieces attached to its two edges so that it can be joined together. ⁸ The artistically woven waistband that is on the ephod must be of one piece, according to the same workmanship of gold, of blue, purple, and scarlet yarn, and of finely spun linen.

⁹ "Take two onyx stones and engrave on them the names of Israel's sons: ¹⁰ six of their names on the first stone and the remaining six names on the second stone, in the order of their birth. ¹¹ Engrave the two stones with the names of Israel's sons as a gem cutter engraves a seal. Mount them, surrounded with gold filigree settings. ¹² Fasten both stones on the shoulder pieces of the ephod as memorial stones for the Israelites. Aaron will carry their names on his two shoulders before the Lord as a reminder. ¹³ Fashion gold filigree settings ¹⁴ and two chains of pure gold; you will make them of braided cord work, and attach the cord chains to the settings.

The Breastpiece

¹⁵ "You are to make an embroidered breastpiece for making decisions. Make it with the same workmanship as the ephod; make it of gold, of blue, purple, and scarlet yarn, and of finely spun linen. ¹⁶ It must be square and folded double, nine inches long and nine inches wide. ¹⁷ Place a setting of gemstones on it, four rows of stones:

The first row should be
a row of carnelian, topaz, and emerald;
¹⁸ the second row,
a turquoise, a lapis lazuli, and a diamond;
¹⁹ the third row,
a jacinth, an agate, and an amethyst;
²⁰ and the fourth row,
a beryl, an onyx, and a jasper.

They should be adorned with gold filigree in their settings. ²¹ The twelve stones are to correspond to the names of Israel's sons. Each stone must be engraved like a seal, with one of the names of the twelve tribes.

²² "You are to make braided chains of pure gold cord work for the breastpiece. ²³ Fashion two gold rings for the breastpiece and attach them to its two corners. ²⁴ Then attach the two gold cords to the two gold rings at the corners of the breastpiece. ²⁵ Attach the other ends of the two cords to the two filigree settings, and in this way attach them to the ephod's shoulder pieces in the front. ²⁶ Make two other gold rings and put them at the two other corners of the breastpiece on the edge that is next to the inner border of the ephod. ²⁷ Make two more gold rings and attach them to the bottom of the ephod's two shoulder pieces on its front, close to its seam, and above the ephod's woven waistband. ²⁸ The artisans are to tie the breastpiece from its rings to the rings of the ephod with a cord of blue yarn, so that the breastpiece is above the ephod's waistband and does not come loose from the ephod.

²⁹ "Whenever he enters the sanctuary,

Aaron is to carry the names of Israel's sons over his heart on the breastpiece for decisions, as a continual reminder before the LORD.

³⁰ Place the Urim and Thummim in the breastpiece for decisions, so that they will also be over Aaron's heart whenever he comes before the LORD. Aaron will continually carry the means of decisions for the Israelites over his heart before the LORD.

"They should use gold; blue, purple, and scarlet yarn; and fine linen."
EXODUS 28:5

Priestly Garments

In Exodus, Aaron becomes Israel's first high priest. His sons were priests who served with him. The high priest represented the people of Israel before God, and his wardrobe was designed to set him apart for this role.

Robe 1

EXODUS 28:31-35; 29:5

A garment woven from blue yarn. The fringe on the lower hem was adorned with alternating gold bells and pomegranates woven from blue, purple, and scarlet yarn. Worn over a specially woven tunic.

Ephod 2

EXODUS 28:6-14, 31

A garment made of woven blue, purple, and scarlet yarn with gold threads woven in to make it shine in the sun.

Sash 3

EXODUS 28:4, 39-40

An embroidered blue, purple, and scarlet belt used to secure the ephod in place and add beauty to the priest's appearance.

Breastplate 4

EXODUS 28:15-21

A thickly woven 9 x 9-inch square that hung from gold shoulder straps. It displayed twelve gemstones engraved with the names of the twelve tribes of Israel.

Shoulder Pieces 5

EXODUS 28:9-10

Gold plates attached to the shoulder straps of the breastplate. An onyx stone was fixed to each plate, with the names of the twelve tribes of Israel engraved on them—six on each shoulder.

Diadem 6

EXODUS 28:36-38

A solid gold medallion bearing the inscription, "HOLY TO THE LORD." Worn over a white linen turban, the diadem was fastened in place with blue yarn.

The Robe

[31] "You are to make the robe of the ephod entirely of blue yarn. [32] There should be an opening at its top in the center of it. Around the opening, there should be a woven collar with an opening like that of body armor so that it does not tear. [33] Make pomegranates of blue, purple, and scarlet yarn on its lower hem and all around it. Put gold bells between them all the way around, [34] so that gold bells and pomegranates alternate around the lower hem of the robe. [35] The robe will be worn by Aaron whenever he ministers, and its sound will be heard when he enters the sanctuary before the LORD and when he exits, so that he does not die.

The Turban

[36] "You are to make a pure gold medallion and engrave it, like the engraving of a seal: HOLY TO THE LORD. [37] Fasten it to a cord of blue yarn so it can be placed on the turban; the medallion is to be on the front of the turban. [38] It will be on Aaron's forehead so that Aaron may bear the guilt connected with the holy offerings that the Israelites consecrate as all their holy gifts. It is always to be on his forehead, so that they may find acceptance with the LORD.

Other Priestly Garments

[39] "You are to weave the tunic from fine linen, make a turban of fine linen, and make an embroidered sash. [40] Make tunics, sashes, and headbands for Aaron's sons to give them glory and beauty. [41] Put these on your brother Aaron and his sons; then anoint, ordain, and consecrate them, so that they may serve me as priests. [42] Make them linen undergarments to cover their naked bodies; they must extend from the waist to the thighs. [43] These must be worn by Aaron and his sons whenever they enter the tent of meeting or approach the altar to minister in the sanctuary area, so that they do not incur guilt and die. This is to be a permanent statute for Aaron and for his future descendants."

Ezekiel 44:15-19, 23-29
The Priests' Duties and Privileges

[15] "But the Levitical priests descended from Zadok, who kept charge of my sanctuary when the Israelites went astray from me, will approach me to serve me. They will stand before me to offer me fat and blood." This is the declaration of the Lord GOD. [16] "They are the ones who may enter my sanctuary and approach my table to serve me. They will keep my mandate. [17] When they enter the gates of the inner court they are to wear linen garments; they must not have on them anything made of wool when they minister at the gates of the inner court and within it. [18] They are to wear linen turbans on their heads and linen undergarments around their waists. They are not to put on anything that makes them sweat. [19] Before they go out to the outer court, to the people, they must take off the clothes they have been ministering in, leave them in the holy chambers, and dress in other clothes so that they do not transmit holiness to the people through their clothes."

...

²³ "They are to teach my people the difference between the holy and the common, and explain to them the difference between the clean and the unclean.

²⁴ "In a dispute, they will officiate as judges and decide the case according to my ordinances. They are to observe my laws and statutes regarding all my appointed festivals, and keep my Sabbaths holy. ²⁵ A priest may not come near a dead person so that he becomes defiled. However, he may defile himself for a father, a mother, a son, a daughter, a brother, or an unmarried sister. ²⁶ After he is cleansed, he is to count off seven days for himself. ²⁷ On the day he goes into the sanctuary, into the inner court to minister in the sanctuary, he is to present his sin offering." This is the declaration of the Lord God.

²⁸ "This will be their inheritance: I am their inheritance.

You are to give them no possession in Israel: I am their possession. ²⁹ They will eat the grain offering, the sin offering, and the guilt offering. Everything in Israel that is permanently dedicated to the Lord will belong to them."

1 Peter 2:4-5

⁴ As you come to him, a living stone—rejected by people but chosen and honored by God— ⁵ you yourselves, as living stones, a spiritual house, are being built to be a holy priesthood to offer spiritual sacrifices acceptable to God through Jesus Christ.

Notes

Day 25
Instructions for Consecration

Exodus 29
Instructions About Consecration

This is what you are to do for them to consecrate them to serve me as priests. Take a young bull and two unblemished rams, ² with unleavened bread, unleavened cakes mixed with oil, and unleavened wafers coated with oil. Make them out of fine wheat flour, ³ put them in a basket, and bring them in the basket, along with the bull and two rams. ⁴ Bring Aaron and his sons to the entrance to the tent of meeting and wash them with water. ⁵ Then take the garments and clothe Aaron with the tunic, the robe for the ephod, the ephod itself, and the breastpiece; fasten the ephod on him with its woven waistband. ⁶ Put the turban on his head and place the holy diadem on the turban. ⁷ Take the anointing oil, pour it on his head, and anoint him. ⁸ You must also bring his sons and clothe them with tunics. ⁹ Tie the sashes on Aaron and his sons and fasten headbands on them. The priesthood is to be theirs by a permanent statute. This is the way you will ordain Aaron and his sons.

¹⁰ "You are to bring the bull to the front of the tent of meeting, and Aaron and his sons must lay their hands on the bull's head. ¹¹ Slaughter the bull before the Lord at the entrance to the tent of meeting. ¹² Take some of the bull's blood and apply it to the horns of the altar with your finger; then pour out all the rest of the blood at the base of the altar. ¹³ Take all the fat that covers the entrails, the fatty lobe of the liver, and the two kidneys with the fat on them, and burn them on the altar. ¹⁴ But burn the bull's flesh, its hide, and its waste outside the camp; it is a sin offering.

¹⁵ "Take one ram, and Aaron and his sons are to lay their hands on the ram's head. ¹⁶ You are to slaughter the ram, take its blood, and splatter it on all sides of the altar. ¹⁷ Cut the ram into pieces. Wash its entrails and legs, and place them with its head

and its pieces on the altar. [18] Then burn the whole ram on the altar; it is a burnt offering to the LORD. It is a pleasing aroma, a fire offering to the LORD.

[19] "You are to take the second ram, and Aaron and his sons must lay their hands on the ram's head. [20] Slaughter the ram, take some of its blood, and put it on Aaron's right earlobe, on his sons' right earlobes, on the thumbs of their right hands, and on the big toes of their right feet. Splatter the remaining blood on all sides of the altar. [21] Take some of the blood that is on the altar and some of the anointing oil, and sprinkle them on Aaron and his garments, as well as on his sons and their garments. So he and his garments will be holy, as well as his sons and their garments.

[22] "Take the fat from the ram, the fat tail, the fat covering the entrails, the fatty lobe of the liver, the two kidneys and the fat on them, and the right thigh (since this is a ram for ordination); [23] take one loaf of bread, one cake of bread made with oil, and one wafer from the basket of unleavened bread that is before the LORD; [24] and put all of them in the hands of Aaron and his sons and present them as a presentation offering before the LORD. [25] Take them from their hands and burn them on the altar on top of the burnt offering, as a pleasing aroma before the LORD; it is a fire offering to the LORD.

[26] "Take the breast from the ram of Aaron's ordination and present it as a presentation offering before the LORD; it is to be your portion. [27] Consecrate for Aaron and his sons the breast of the presentation offering that is presented and the thigh of the contribution that is lifted up from the ram of ordination. [28] This will belong to Aaron and his sons as a regular portion from the Israelites, for it is a contribution. It will be the Israelites' contribution from their fellowship sacrifices, their contribution to the LORD.

[29] "The holy garments that belong to Aaron are to belong to his sons after him, so that they can be anointed and ordained in them. [30] Any priest who is one of his sons and who succeeds him and enters the tent of meeting to minister in the sanctuary must wear them for seven days.

[31] "You are to take the ram of ordination and boil its flesh in a holy place. [32] Aaron and his sons are to eat the meat of the ram and the bread that is in the basket at the entrance to the tent of meeting. [33] They must eat those things by which atonement was made at the time of their ordination and consecration. An unauthorized person must not eat them, for these things are holy. [34] If any of the meat of ordination or any of the bread is left until morning, burn what is left over. It must not be eaten because it is holy.

[35] "This is what you are to do for Aaron and his sons based on all I have commanded you. Take seven days to ordain them. [36] Sacrifice a bull as a sin offering each day for atonement. Purify the altar when you make atonement for it, and anoint it in order to consecrate it. [37] For seven days you must make atonement for the altar and consecrate it. The altar will be especially holy. Whatever touches the altar will be consecrated.

[38] "This is what you are to offer regularly on the altar every day: two year-old lambs. [39] In the morning offer one lamb, and at twilight offer the other lamb. [40] With the first lamb offer two quarts of fine flour mixed with one quart of oil from crushed olives, and a drink offering of one quart of wine. [41] You are to offer the second lamb at twilight. Offer a grain offering and a drink offering with it, like the one in the morning, as a pleasing aroma, a fire offering to the LORD. [42] This will be a regular burnt offering throughout your generations at the entrance to the tent of meeting before the LORD, where I will meet you to speak with you. [43] I will also meet with the Israelites there, and that place will be consecrated by my glory. [44] I will consecrate the tent of meeting and the altar; I will also consecrate Aaron and his sons to serve me as priests.

[45] I will dwell among the Israelites and be their God.

"The priesthood is to be theirs by a permanent statute." EXODUS 29:9

46 And they will know that I am the LORD their God, who brought them out of the land of Egypt, so that I might dwell among them. I am the LORD their God."

Psalm 132:12-16

12 "If your sons keep my covenant
and my decrees that I will teach them,
their sons will also sit on your throne forever."

13 For the LORD has chosen Zion;
he has desired it for his home:
14 "This is my resting place forever;
I will make my home here
because I have desired it.
15 I will abundantly bless its food;
I will satisfy its needy with bread.
16 I will clothe its priests with salvation,
and its faithful people will shout for joy."

Hebrews 7:23-28

23 Now many have become Levitical priests, since they are prevented by death from remaining in office. 24 But because he remains forever, he holds his priesthood permanently. 25 Therefore, he is able to save completely those who come to God through him, since he always lives to intercede for them.

26 For this is the kind of high priest we need: holy, innocent, undefiled, separated from sinners, and exalted above the heavens. 27 He doesn't need to offer sacrifices every day, as high priests do—first for their own sins, then for those of the people. He did this once for all time when he offered himself. 28 For the law appoints as high priests men who are weak, but the promise of the oath, which came after the law, appoints a Son, who has been perfected forever.

Notes

Day 26
The Incense Altar

Exodus 30
The Incense Altar

You are to make an altar for the burning of incense; make it of acacia wood. ² It must be square, eighteen inches long and eighteen inches wide; it must be thirty-six inches high. Its horns must be of one piece with it. ³ Overlay its top, all around its sides, and its horns with pure gold; make a gold molding all around it. ⁴ Make two gold rings for it under the molding on two of its sides; put these on opposite sides of it to be holders for the poles to carry it with. ⁵ Make the poles of acacia wood and overlay them with gold.

⁶ "You are to place the altar in front of the curtain by the ark of the testimony—in front of the mercy seat that is over the testimony—where I will meet with you. ⁷ Aaron must burn fragrant incense on it; he must burn it every morning when he tends the lamps. ⁸ When Aaron sets up the lamps at twilight, he must burn incense. There is to be an incense offering before the LORD throughout your generations. ⁹ You must not offer unauthorized incense on it, or a burnt or grain offering; you are not to pour a drink offering on it.

¹⁰ "Once a year Aaron is to perform the atonement ceremony for the altar. Throughout your generations he is to perform the atonement ceremony for it once a year, with the blood of the sin offering for atonement on the horns. The altar is especially holy to the LORD."

The Atonement Money

¹¹ The LORD spoke to Moses: ¹² "When you take a census of the Israelites to register them, each of the men must pay a ransom for his life to the LORD as they are registered. Then no plague will come on them as they are registered. ¹³ Everyone who is registered must pay half a shekel according to the sanctuary shekel (twenty gerahs

to the shekel). This half shekel is a contribution to the LORD. ¹⁴ Each man who is registered, twenty years old or more, must give this contribution to the LORD. ¹⁵ The wealthy may not give more and the poor may not give less than half a shekel when giving the contribution to the LORD to atone for your lives. ¹⁶ Take the atonement price from the Israelites and use it for the service of the tent of meeting. It will serve as a reminder for the Israelites before the LORD to atone for your lives."

The Bronze Basin

¹⁷ The LORD spoke to Moses: ¹⁸ "Make a bronze basin for washing and a bronze stand for it. Set it between the tent of meeting and the altar, and put water in it. ¹⁹ Aaron and his sons must wash their hands and feet from the basin. ²⁰ Whenever they enter the tent of meeting or approach the altar to minister by burning an offering to the LORD, they must wash with water so that they will not die. ²¹ They must wash their hands and feet so that they will not die; this is to be a permanent statute for them, for Aaron and his descendants throughout their generations."

The Anointing Oil

²² The LORD spoke to Moses: ²³ "Take for yourself the finest spices: 12½ pounds of liquid myrrh, half as much (6¼ pounds) of fragrant cinnamon, 6¼ pounds of fragrant cane, ²⁴ 12½ pounds of cassia (by the sanctuary shekel), and a gallon of olive oil. ²⁵ Prepare from these a holy anointing oil, a scented blend, the work of a perfumer; it will be holy anointing oil.

²⁶ "With it you are to anoint the tent of meeting, the ark of the testimony, ²⁷ the table with all its utensils, the lampstand with its utensils, the altar of incense, ²⁸ the altar of burnt offering with all its utensils, and the basin with its stand. ²⁹ Consecrate them and they will be especially holy. Whatever touches them will be consecrated. ³⁰ Anoint Aaron and his sons and consecrate them to serve me as priests.

³¹ "Tell the Israelites: This will be my holy anointing oil throughout your generations. ³² It must not be used for ordinary anointing on a person's body, and you must not make anything like it using its formula. It is holy, and it must be holy to you. ³³ Anyone who blends something like it or puts some of it on an unauthorized person must be cut off from his people."

The Sacred Incense

³⁴ The LORD said to Moses: "Take fragrant spices: stacte, onycha, and galbanum; the spices and pure frankincense are to be in equal measures. ³⁵ Prepare expertly blended incense from these; it is to be seasoned with salt, pure and holy. ³⁶ Grind some of it into a fine powder and put some in front of the testimony in the tent of meeting, where I will meet with you. It must be especially holy to you. ³⁷ As for the incense you are making, you must not make any for yourselves using its formula. It is to be regarded by you as holy—belonging to the LORD. ³⁸ Anyone who makes something like it to smell its fragrance must be cut off from his people."

"The altar is especially holy to the LORD." EXODUS 30:10

2 Corinthians 2:14-16

A Ministry of Life or Death

14 But thanks be to God, who always leads us in Christ's triumphal procession and through us spreads the aroma of the knowledge of him in every place. 15 For to God we are the fragrance of Christ among those who are being saved and among those who are perishing. 16 To some we are an aroma of death leading to death, but to others, an aroma of life leading to life. Who is adequate for these things?

1 John 2:24-27

Remaining with God

24 What you have heard from the beginning is to remain in you. If what you have heard from the beginning remains in you, then you will remain in the Son and in the Father. 25 And this is the promise that he himself made to us: eternal life.

26 I have written these things to you concerning those who are trying to deceive you. 27 As for you, the anointing you received from him remains in you, and you don't need anyone to teach you. Instead, his anointing teaches you about all things and is true and is not a lie; just as it has taught you, remain in him.

Month   Day

Notes

Day 27
Grace Day

Use today to pray, rest, and reflect on this week's reading, giving thanks for the grace that is ours in Christ.

But because he remains forever, he holds his priesthood permanently. Therefore, he is able to save completely those who come to God through him, since he always lives to intercede for them.

HEBREWS 7:24-25

ALMOND SQUARE INGREDIENTS

2 medium tangerines or clementines

3 tablespoons orange juice

4 tablespoons cashew milk

2 tablespoons flax meal

2 tablespoons tapioca flour

½ cup sugar

1 teaspoon almond extract

½ teaspoon orange flavoring

1½ cups natural almond flour

1 tablespoon coconut flour

1 teaspoon baking powder

GLAZE INGREDIENTS

½ cup shredded coconut

1 cup powdered sugar

2 tablespoons orange juice

1 teaspoon almond extract

½ teaspoon orange flavoring

OPTIONAL INGREDIENTS

Orange zest, for garnish

Almond slivers, for garnish

Almond Squares with Toasted Coconut Glaze

TOTAL TIME: 2 HOURS

SERVES: 2

DIRECTIONS

Preheat oven to 350°F.

Place tangerines—with the peels still on—in a pan, and cover with cold water. Bring to a boil and let simmer for 15 minutes. Drain the hot water and re-cover the tangerines with cold water. Bring to a boil again and simmer for another 15 minutes.

Place the softened tangerines on a plate and cut. Remove any seeds, then blend peels and pulp in a food processor until smooth.

Combine orange juice, cashew milk, flax meal, and tapioca flour in a mixing bowl, giving it a brisk stir, then set aside to thicken. Add tangerine puree, sugar, almond extract, and orange flavoring to mixture.

In a separate mixing bowl, quickly whisk almond flour, coconut flour, and baking powder. Combine the two bowls and stir thoroughly.

Pour into a buttered and floured 9x9 baking pan, working to spread the stiff mixture evenly into all corners.

Bake 45-50 minutes until firm.

Allow bars to briefly cool before transferring to a serving tray. Top with glaze, orange zest, and almond slivers.

GLAZE DIRECTIONS

Place shredded coconut on a baking sheet and bake for 10 minutes, redistributing halfway through.

Whisk powdered sugar, orange juice, almond extract, and orange flavoring in a bowl. Drizzle over almond bars.

Day 28
Weekly Truth

"They are to make a sanctuary for me so that I may dwell among them."

EXODUS 25:8

Scripture is God-breathed and true. When we memorize it, we carry the gospel with us wherever we go.

This week's verse reminds us of the significance of the detailed instructions God gave for building the tabernacle.

Find the corresponding memory card in the back of your book.

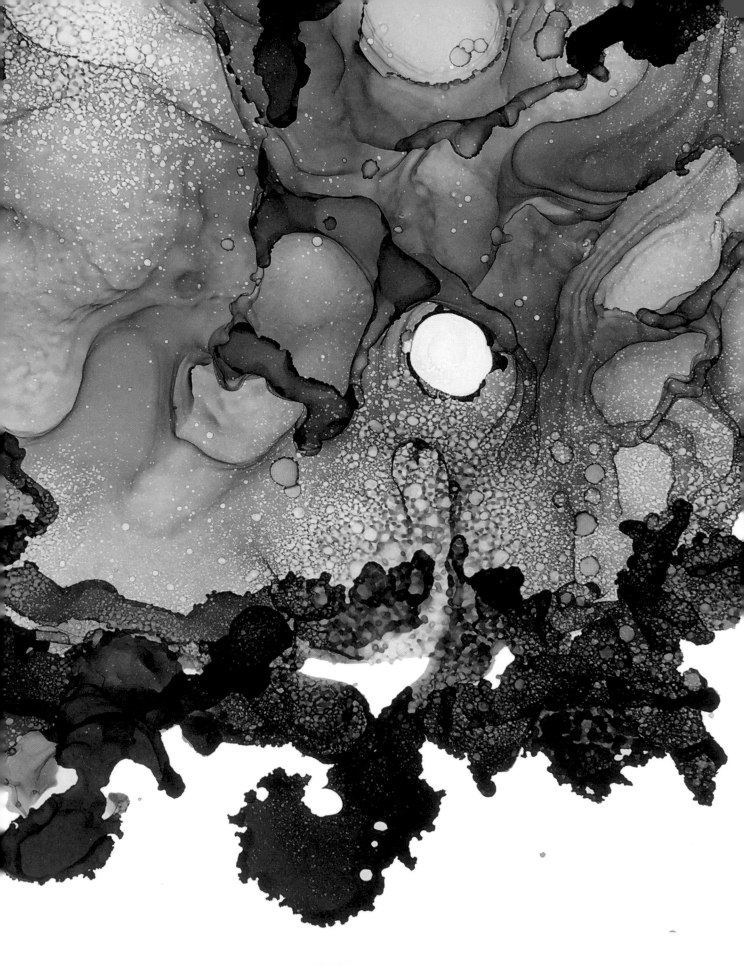

Day 29
The Skilled Workers

Exodus 31
God's Provision of the Skilled Workers

The LORD also spoke to Moses: [2] "Look, I have appointed by name Bezalel son of Uri, son of Hur, of the tribe of Judah. [3] I have filled him with God's Spirit, with wisdom, understanding, and ability in every craft [4] to design artistic works in gold, silver, and bronze, [5] to cut gemstones for mounting, and to carve wood for work in every craft. [6] I have also selected Oholiab son of Ahisamach, of the tribe of Dan, to be with him. I have put wisdom in the heart of every skilled artisan in order to make all that I have commanded you: [7] the tent of meeting, the ark of the testimony, the mercy seat that is on top of it, and all the other furnishings of the tent— [8] the table with its utensils, the pure gold lampstand with all its utensils, the altar of incense, [9] the altar of burnt offering with all its utensils, the basin with its stand— [10] the specially woven garments, both the holy garments for the priest Aaron and the garments for his sons to serve as priests, [11] the anointing oil, and the fragrant incense for the sanctuary. They must make them according to all that I have commanded you."

Observing the Sabbath

[12] The LORD said to Moses: [13] "Tell the Israelites: You must observe my Sabbaths, for it is a sign between me and you throughout your generations, so that you will know that I am the LORD who consecrates you. [14] Observe the Sabbath, for it is holy to you. Whoever profanes it must be put to death. If anyone does work on it, that person must be cut off from his people. [15] Work may be done for six days, but on the seventh day there must be a Sabbath of complete rest, holy to the LORD. Anyone who does work on the Sabbath day must be put to death. [16] The Israelites must observe the Sabbath, celebrating it throughout their generations as a permanent covenant. [17] It is a sign forever between me and the Israelites, for in six days the LORD made the heavens and the earth, but on the seventh day he rested and was refreshed."

The Two Stone Tablets

¹⁸ When he finished speaking with Moses on Mount Sinai, he gave him the two tablets of the testimony, stone tablets inscribed by the finger of God.

Jeremiah 31:31-34
The New Covenant

³¹ "Look, the days are coming"—this is the LORD's declaration—"when I will make a new covenant with the house of Israel and with the house of Judah. ³² This one will not be like the covenant I made with their ancestors on the day I took them by the hand to lead them out of the land of Egypt—my covenant that they broke even though I am their master"—the LORD's declaration. ³³ "Instead, this is the covenant I will make with the house of Israel after those days"—the LORD's declaration. "I will put my teaching within them and write it on their hearts. I will be their God, and they will be my people. ³⁴ No longer will one teach his neighbor or his brother, saying, 'Know the LORD,' for they will all know me, from the least to the greatest of them"—this is the LORD's declaration. "For I will forgive their iniquity and never again remember their sin."

2 Corinthians 3:1-3
Living Letters

¹ Are we beginning to commend ourselves again? Or do we need, like some, letters of recommendation to you or from you? ² You yourselves are our letter, written on our hearts, known and read by everyone. ³ You show that you are Christ's letter, delivered by us, not written with ink but with the Spirit of the living God—not on tablets of stone but on tablets of human hearts.

Hymn
Praise to the Lord, the Almighty

Text: Joachim Neander, 1680
Tune: German folk tune
Original English Translation: Catherine Winkworth, 1863

Praise to the Lord, the Almighty, the King of creation!
O my soul, praise Him, for He is your health and salvation!
Come, all who hear; now to His temple draw near,
join me in glad adoration.

Praise to the Lord, above all things so wondrously reigning;
sheltering you under His wings, and so gently sustaining!
Have you not seen all that is needful has been
sent by His gracious ordaining?

Praise to the Lord, who will prosper your work and defend you;
surely His goodness and mercy shall daily attend you.
Ponder anew what the Almighty can do,
if with His love He befriends you.

Praise to the Lord! O let all that is in me adore Him!
All that has life and breath, come now with praises before Him.
Let the amen sound from His people again;
gladly forever adore Him.

Bella and Broth
Noodle Bowl

TOTAL TIME: 30 MINUTES

SERVES: 2

DIRECTIONS

Sauté shallot with a drizzle of olive oil in a large skillet over medium heat for 4 minutes. Add garlic and stir together for 1 minute. Add miso paste, curry paste, harissa, and lime juice, mixing until fully incorporated and thick.

Add mushrooms and stir until they begin to soften, then add vegetable broth and coconut milk. Simmer until broth is fully heated and incorporated.

Add rice noodles to broth. Top with dried cilantro and serve.

Day 30
The Gold Calf

Exodus 32
The Gold Calf

When the people saw that Moses delayed in coming down from the mountain, they gathered around Aaron and said to him, "Come, make gods for us who will go before us because this Moses, the man who brought us up from the land of Egypt—we don't know what has happened to him!"

2 Aaron replied to them, "Take off the gold rings that are on the ears of your wives, your sons, and your daughters and bring them to me." 3 So all the people took off the gold rings that were on their ears and brought them to Aaron. 4 He took the gold from them, fashioned it with an engraving tool, and made it into an image of a calf.

Then they said, "Israel, these are your gods, who brought you up from the land of Egypt!"

5 When Aaron saw this, he built an altar in front of it and made an announcement: "There will be a festival to the LORD tomorrow." 6 Early the next morning they arose, offered burnt offerings, and presented fellowship offerings. The people sat down to eat and drink, and got up to party.

7 The LORD spoke to Moses: "Go down at once! For your people you brought up from the land of Egypt have acted corruptly. 8 They have quickly turned from the way I commanded them; they have made for themselves an image of a calf. They have bowed down to it, sacrificed to it, and said, 'Israel, these are your gods, who brought you up from the land of Egypt.'" 9 The LORD also said to Moses: "I have

seen this people, and they are indeed a stiff-necked people. [10] Now leave me alone, so that my anger can burn against them and I can destroy them. Then I will make you into a great nation."

[11] But Moses sought the favor of the LORD his God: "LORD, why does your anger burn against your people you brought out of the land of Egypt with great power and a strong hand? [12] Why should the Egyptians say, 'He brought them out with an evil intent to kill them in the mountains and eliminate them from the face of the earth'? Turn from your fierce anger and relent concerning this disaster planned for your people. [13] Remember your servants Abraham, Isaac, and Israel—you swore to them by yourself and declared, 'I will make your offspring as numerous as the stars of the sky and will give your offspring all this land that I have promised, and they will inherit it forever.'" [14] So the LORD relented concerning the disaster he had said he would bring on his people.

[15] Then Moses turned and went down the mountain with the two tablets of the testimony in his hands. They were inscribed on both sides—inscribed front and back. [16] The tablets were the work of God, and the writing was God's writing, engraved on the tablets.

[17] When Joshua heard the sound of the people as they shouted, he said to Moses, "There is a sound of war in the camp."

[18] But Moses replied:

It's not the sound of a victory cry
and not the sound of a cry of defeat;
I hear the sound of singing!

[19] As he approached the camp and saw the calf and the dancing, Moses became enraged and threw the tablets out of his hands, smashing them at the base of the mountain. [20] He took the calf they had made, burned it up, and ground it to powder. He scattered the powder over the surface of the water and forced the Israelites to drink the water.

[21] Then Moses asked Aaron,

"What did these people do to you that you have led them into such a grave sin?"

[22] "Don't be enraged, my lord," Aaron replied. "You yourself know that the people are intent on evil. [23] They said to me, 'Make gods for us who will go before us because this Moses, the man who brought us up from the land of Egypt—we don't know what has happened to him!' [24] So I said to them, 'Whoever has gold, take it off,' and they gave it to me. When I threw it into the fire, out came this calf!"

"I have seen this people, and they are indeed a stiff-necked people."
EXODUS 32:9

²⁵ Moses saw that the people were out of control, for Aaron had let them get out of control, making them a laughingstock to their enemies. ²⁶ And Moses stood at the camp's entrance and said, "Whoever is for the Lord, come to me." And all the Levites gathered around him. ²⁷ He told them, "This is what the Lord, the God of Israel, says, 'Every man fasten his sword to his side; go back and forth through the camp from entrance to entrance, and each of you kill his brother, his friend, and his neighbor.'" ²⁸ The Levites did as Moses commanded, and about three thousand men fell dead that day among the people. ²⁹ Afterward Moses said, "Today you have been dedicated to the Lord, since each man went against his son and his brother. Therefore you have brought a blessing on yourselves today."

³⁰ The following day Moses said to the people, "You have committed a grave sin. Now I will go up to the Lord; perhaps I will be able to atone for your sin."

³¹ So Moses returned to the Lord and said, "Oh, these people have committed a grave sin; they have made a god of gold for themselves. ³² Now if you would only forgive their sin. But if not, please erase me from the book you have written."

³³ The Lord replied to Moses: "Whoever has sinned against me I will erase from my book. ³⁴ Now go, lead the people to the place I told you about; see, my angel will go before you. But on the day I settle accounts, I will hold them accountable for their sin." ³⁵ And the Lord inflicted a plague on the people for what they did with the calf Aaron had made.

1 Kings 12:26-28

²⁶ Jeroboam said to himself, "The kingdom might now return to the house of David. ²⁷ If these people regularly go to offer sacrifices in the Lord's temple in Jerusalem, the heart of these people will return to their lord, King Rehoboam of Judah. They will kill me and go back to the king of Judah." ²⁸ So the king sought advice.

Then he made two golden calves, and he said to the people, "Going to Jerusalem is too difficult for you. Israel, here are your gods who brought you up from the land of Egypt."

Notes

Day 31
The Lord's Glory

Exodus 33

The Tent Outside the Camp

The LORD spoke to Moses: "Go up from here, you and the people you brought up from the land of Egypt, to the land I promised to Abraham, Isaac, and Jacob, saying: I will give it to your offspring. [2] I will send an angel ahead of you and will drive out the Canaanites, Amorites, Hethites, Perizzites, Hivites, and Jebusites. [3] Go up to a land flowing with milk and honey. But I will not go up with you because you are a stiff-necked people; otherwise, I might destroy you on the way." [4] When the people heard this bad news, they mourned and didn't put on their jewelry.

[5] For the LORD said to Moses: "Tell the Israelites: You are a stiff-necked people. If I went up with you for a single moment, I would destroy you. Now take off your jewelry, and I will decide what to do with you." [6] So the Israelites remained stripped of their jewelry from Mount Horeb onward.

[7] Now Moses took a tent and pitched it outside the camp, at a distance from the camp; he called it the tent of meeting. Anyone who wanted to consult the LORD would go to the tent of meeting that was outside the camp. [8] Whenever Moses went out to the tent, all the people would stand up, each one at the door of his tent, and they would watch Moses until he entered the tent. [9] When Moses entered the tent, the pillar of cloud would come down and remain at the entrance to the tent, and the LORD would speak with Moses. [10] As all the people saw the pillar of cloud remaining at the entrance to the tent, they would stand up, then bow in worship, each one at the door of his tent. [11] The LORD would speak with Moses face to face, just as a man speaks with his friend, then Moses would return to the camp. His assistant, the young man Joshua son of Nun, would not leave the inside of the tent.

The Lord's Glory

[12] Moses said to the LORD, "Look, you have told me, 'Lead this people up,' but you have not let me know whom you will send with me. You said, 'I know you by name, and you have also found favor with me.' [13] Now if I have indeed found favor with you, please teach me your ways, and I will know you, so that I may find favor with you. Now consider that this nation is your people."

[14] And he replied, "My presence will go with you, and I will give you rest."

[15] "If your presence does not go," Moses responded to him, "don't make us go up from here. [16] How will it be known that I and your people have found favor with you unless you go with us? I and your people will be distinguished by this from all the other people on the face of the earth."

[17] The LORD answered Moses, "I will do this very thing you have asked, for you have found favor with me, and I know you by name."

[18] Then Moses said, "Please, let me see your glory."

[19] He said,

"I will cause all my goodness to pass in front of you, and I will proclaim the name 'the LORD' before you.

I will be gracious to whom I will be gracious, and I will have compassion on whom I will have compassion." [20] But he added, "You cannot see my face, for humans cannot see me and live." [21] The LORD said, "Here is a place near me. You are to stand on the rock, [22] and when my glory passes by, I will put you in the crevice of the rock and cover you with my hand until I have passed by. [23] Then I will take my hand away, and you will see my back, but my face will not be seen."

Genesis 3:8-10
Sin's Consequences

[8] Then the man and his wife heard the sound of the LORD God walking in the garden at the time of the evening breeze, and they hid from the LORD God among the trees of the garden. [9] So the LORD God called out to the man and said to him, "Where are you?"

[10] And he said, "I heard you in the garden, and I was afraid because I was naked, so I hid."

Numbers 6:22-26
The Priestly Blessing

[22] The LORD spoke to Moses: [23] "Tell Aaron and his sons, 'This is how you are to bless the Israelites. You should say to them,

[24] "May the LORD bless you and protect you;
[25] may the LORD make his face shine on you
and be gracious to you;
[26] may the LORD look with favor on you
and give you peace."'"

Day 32
Moses' Radiant Face

Exodus 34
New Stone Tablets

The LORD said to Moses, "Cut two stone tablets like the first ones, and I will write on them the words that were on the first tablets, which you broke. ² Be prepared by morning. Come up Mount Sinai in the morning and stand before me on the mountaintop. ³ No one may go up with you; in fact, no one should be seen anywhere on the mountain. Even the flocks and herds are not to graze in front of that mountain."

⁴ Moses cut two stone tablets like the first ones. He got up early in the morning, and taking the two stone tablets in his hand, he climbed Mount Sinai, just as the LORD had commanded him.

⁵ The LORD came down in a cloud, stood with him there, and proclaimed his name, "the LORD." ⁶ The LORD passed in front of him and proclaimed:

The LORD—the LORD is a compassionate and gracious God, slow to anger and abounding in faithful love and truth, ⁷ maintaining faithful love to a thousand generations, forgiving iniquity, rebellion, and sin. But he will not leave the guilty unpunished, bringing the fathers' iniquity on the children and grandchildren to the third and fourth generation.

⁸ Moses immediately knelt low on the ground and worshiped. ⁹ Then he said, "My Lord, if I have indeed found favor with you, my Lord, please go with us (even though this is a stiff-necked people), forgive our iniquity and our sin, and accept us as your own possession."

Covenant Obligations

¹⁰ And the LORD responded: "Look, I am making a covenant. I will perform wonders in the presence of all your people that have never been done in the whole earth or in any nation. All the people you live among will see the LORD's work, for what I am doing with you is awe-inspiring. ¹¹ Observe what I command you today. I am going to drive out before you the Amorites, Canaanites, Hethites, Perizzites, Hivites, and Jebusites. ¹² Be careful not to make a treaty with the inhabitants of the land that you are going to enter; otherwise, they will become a snare among you. ¹³ Instead, you must tear down their altars, smash their sacred pillars, and chop down their Asherah poles. ¹⁴ Because the LORD is jealous for his reputation, you are never to bow down to another god. He is a jealous God.

¹⁵ "Do not make a treaty with the inhabitants of the land, or else when they prostitute themselves with their gods and sacrifice to their gods, they will invite you, and you will eat their sacrifices. ¹⁶ Then you will take some of their daughters as brides for your sons. Their daughters will prostitute themselves with their gods and cause your sons to prostitute themselves with their gods.

¹⁷ "Do not make cast images of gods for yourselves.

¹⁸ "Observe the Festival of Unleavened Bread. You are to eat unleavened bread for seven days at the appointed time in the month of Abib, as I commanded you, for you came out of Egypt in the month of Abib.

¹⁹ "The firstborn male from every womb belongs to me, including all your male livestock, the firstborn of cattle or sheep. ²⁰ You may redeem the firstborn of a donkey with a sheep, but if you do not redeem it, break its neck. You must redeem all the firstborn of your sons. No one is to appear before me empty-handed.

²¹ "You are to labor six days but you must rest on the seventh day; you must even rest during plowing and harvesting times.

²² "Observe the Festival of Weeks with the firstfruits of the wheat harvest, and the Festival of Ingathering at the turn of the agricultural year. ²³ Three times a year all your males are to appear before the Lord GOD, the God of Israel. ²⁴ For I will drive out nations before you and enlarge your territory. No one will covet your land when you go up three times a year to appear before the LORD your God.

²⁵ "Do not present the blood for my sacrifice with anything leavened. The sacrifice of the Passover Festival must not remain until morning.

²⁶ "Bring the best firstfruits of your land to the house of the LORD your God.

"You must not boil a young goat in its mother's milk."

"All the people you live among will see the LORD's work, for what I am doing with you is awe-inspiring." EXODUS 34:10

²⁷ The LORD also said to Moses, "Write down these words, for I have made a covenant with you and with Israel based on these words."

²⁸ Moses was there with the LORD forty days and forty nights; he did not eat food or drink water. He wrote the Ten Commandments, the words of the covenant, on the tablets.

Moses's Radiant Face

²⁹ As Moses descended from Mount Sinai—with the two tablets of the testimony in his hands as he descended the mountain—he did not realize that the skin of his face shone as a result of his speaking with the LORD. ³⁰ When Aaron and all the Israelites saw Moses, the skin of his face shone! They were afraid to come near him. ³¹ But Moses called out to them, so Aaron and all the leaders of the community returned to him, and Moses spoke to them. ³² Afterward all the Israelites came near, and he commanded them to do everything the LORD had told him on Mount Sinai. ³³ When Moses had finished speaking with them, he put a veil over his face. ³⁴ But whenever Moses went before the LORD to speak with him, he would remove the veil until he came out. After he came out, he would tell the Israelites what he had been commanded,

³⁵ and the Israelites would see that Moses's face was radiant.

Then Moses would put the veil over his face again until he went to speak with the LORD.

John 14:8-11
Jesus Reveals the Father

⁸ "Lord," said Philip, "show us the Father, and that's enough for us."

⁹ Jesus said to him, "Have I been among you all this time and you do not know me, Philip? The one who has seen me has seen the Father. How can you say, 'Show us the Father'? ¹⁰ Don't you believe that I am in the Father and the Father is in me? The words I speak to you I do not speak on my own.

The Father who lives in me does his works. ¹¹ Believe me that I am in the Father and the Father is in me. Otherwise, believe because of the works themselves."

2 Corinthians 3:12-18

¹² Since, then, we have such a hope, we act with great boldness.

¹³ We are not like Moses, who used to put a veil over his face to prevent the Israelites from gazing steadily until the end of the glory of what was being set aside, ¹⁴ but their minds were hardened. For to this day, at the reading of the old covenant, the same veil remains; it is not lifted, because it is set aside only in Christ. ¹⁵ Yet still today, whenever Moses is read, a veil lies over their hearts, ¹⁶ but whenever a person turns to the Lord, the veil is removed. ¹⁷ Now the Lord is the Spirit, and where the Spirit of the Lord is, there is freedom. ¹⁸ We all, with unveiled faces, are looking as in a mirror at the glory of the Lord and are being transformed into the same image from glory to glory; this is from the Lord who is the Spirit.

Notes

Day 33
Offerings to Build the Tabernacle

Exodus 35
The Sabbath Command

Moses assembled the entire Israelite community and said to them, "These are the things that the Lord has commanded you to do: ² For six days work is to be done, but on the seventh day you are to have a holy day, a Sabbath of complete rest to the Lord. Anyone who does work on it must be executed. ³ Do not light a fire in any of your homes on the Sabbath day."

Building the Tabernacle

⁴ Then Moses said to the entire Israelite community, "This is what the Lord has commanded: ⁵ Take up an offering among you for the Lord. Let everyone whose heart is willing bring this as the Lord's offering: gold, silver, and bronze; ⁶ blue, purple, and scarlet yarn; fine linen and goat hair; ⁷ ram skins dyed red and fine leather; acacia wood; ⁸ oil for the light; spices for the anointing oil and for the fragrant incense; ⁹ and onyx with gemstones to mount on the ephod and breastpiece.

¹⁰ "Let all the skilled artisans among you come and make everything that the Lord has commanded: ¹¹ the tabernacle—its tent and covering, its clasps and supports, its crossbars, its pillars and bases; ¹² the ark with its poles, the mercy seat, and the curtain for the screen; ¹³ the table with its poles, all its utensils, and the Bread of the Presence; ¹⁴ the lampstand for light with its utensils and lamps as well as the oil for the light; ¹⁵ the altar of incense with its poles; the anointing oil and the fragrant incense; the entryway screen for the entrance to the tabernacle; ¹⁶ the altar of burnt offering with its bronze grate, its poles, and all its utensils; the basin with its stand; ¹⁷ the hangings of the courtyard, its posts and bases, and the screen for the gate of the courtyard; ¹⁸ the tent pegs for the tabernacle and the tent pegs for the courtyard, along with their ropes; ¹⁹ and the specially woven garments for ministering in the

sanctuary—the holy garments for the priest Aaron and the garments for his sons to serve as priests."

20 Then the entire Israelite community left Moses's presence. 21 Everyone whose heart was moved and whose spirit prompted him came and brought an offering to the LORD for the work on the tent of meeting, for all its services, and for the holy garments. 22 Both men and women came; all who had willing hearts brought brooches, earrings, rings, necklaces, and all kinds of gold jewelry—everyone who presented a presentation offering of gold to the LORD. 23 Everyone who possessed blue, purple, or scarlet yarn, fine linen or goat hair, ram skins dyed red or fine leather, brought them. 24 Everyone making an offering of silver or bronze brought it as a contribution to the LORD. Everyone who possessed acacia wood useful for any task in the work brought it. 25 Every skilled woman spun yarn with her hands and brought it: blue, purple, and scarlet yarn, and fine linen. 26 And all the women whose hearts were moved spun the goat hair by virtue of their skill. 27 The leaders brought onyx and gemstones to mount on the ephod and breastpiece, 28 as well as the spice and oil for the light, for the anointing oil, and for the fragrant incense. 29 So the Israelites brought a freewill offering to the LORD, all the men and women whose hearts prompted them to bring something for all the work that the LORD, through Moses, had commanded to be done.

Bezalel and Oholiab

30 Moses then said to the Israelites: "Look, the LORD has appointed by name Bezalel son of Uri, son of Hur, of the tribe of Judah. 31 He has filled him with God's Spirit, with wisdom, understanding, and ability in every kind of craft 32 to design artistic works in gold, silver, and bronze, 33 to cut gemstones for mounting, and to carve wood for work in every kind of artistic craft. 34 He has also given both him and Oholiab son of Ahisamach, of the tribe of Dan, the ability to teach others. 35 He has filled them with skill to do all the work of a gem cutter; a designer; an embroiderer in blue, purple, and scarlet yarn and fine linen; and a weaver. They can do every kind of craft and design artistic designs."

John 10:17-18

17 "This is why the Father loves me, because I lay down my life so that I may take it up again. 18 No one takes it from me, but I lay it down on my own. I have the right to lay it down, and I have the right to take it up again. I have received this command from my Father."

Romans 12:1
A Living Sacrifice

Therefore, brothers and sisters, in view of the mercies of God, I urge you to present your bodies as a living sacrifice, holy and pleasing to God; this is your true worship.

Day 34
Grace Day

Use today to pray, rest, and reflect on this week's reading, giving thanks for the grace that is ours in Christ.

Now the Lord is the Spirit, and where the Spirit of the Lord is, there is freedom. We all, with unveiled faces, are looking as in a mirror at the glory of the Lord and are being transformed into the same image from glory to glory; this is from the Lord who is the Spirit.

2 CORINTHIANS 3:17-18

INGREDIENTS

1 shallot, sliced

Drizzle of olive oil

1 tablespoon garlic

1 tablespoon chickpea miso paste

2 tablespoons red curry paste

1 teaspoon harissa

2 teaspoons lime juice

5 large or 8 medium baby portabella mushrooms, sliced

2 cups vegetable broth

7 ounces lite coconut milk

Handful of maifun brown rice noodles

½ teaspoon dried cilantro

Day 35
Weekly Truth

"The LORD is a compassionate and gracious God,
slow to anger and abounding in faithful love and truth,
maintaining faithful love to a thousand generations,
forgiving iniquity, rebellion, and sin."

EXODUS 34:6-7

Scripture is God-breathed and true. When we memorize it, we carry the gospel with us wherever we go.

This week's verse is the Lord's own description of Himself to His people.

Find the corresponding memory card in the back of your book.

Day 36
Building the Tabernacle

Exodus 36

Bezalel, Oholiab, and all the skilled people are to work based on everything the LORD has commanded. The LORD has given them wisdom and understanding to know how to do all the work of constructing the sanctuary."

² So Moses summoned Bezalel, Oholiab, and every skilled person in whose heart the LORD had placed wisdom, all whose hearts moved them, to come to the work and do it. ³ They took from Moses's presence all the contributions that the Israelites had brought for the task of making the sanctuary. Meanwhile, the people continued to bring freewill offerings morning after morning.

⁴ Then all the artisans who were doing all the work for the sanctuary came one by one from the work they were doing ⁵ and said to Moses, "The people are bringing more than is needed for the construction of the work the LORD commanded to be done."

⁶ After Moses gave an order, they sent a proclamation throughout the camp: "Let no man or woman make anything else as an offering for the sanctuary." So the people stopped. ⁷ The materials were sufficient for them to do all the work. There was more than enough.

Building the Tabernacle

⁸ All the skilled artisans among those doing the work made the tabernacle with ten curtains. Bezalel made them of finely spun linen, as well as blue, purple, and scarlet yarn, with a design of cherubim worked into them. ⁹ Each curtain was forty-two feet long and six feet wide; all the curtains had the same measurements. ¹⁰ He joined five of the curtains to each other, and the other five curtains he joined to each other. ¹¹ He made loops of blue yarn on the edge of the last curtain in the first set and did

the same on the edge of the outermost curtain in the second set. ¹² He made fifty loops on the one curtain and fifty loops on the edge of the curtain in the second set, so that the loops lined up with each other. ¹³ He also made fifty gold clasps and joined the curtains to each other, so that the tabernacle became a single unit.

¹⁴ He made curtains of goat hair for a tent over the tabernacle; he made eleven of them. ¹⁵ Each curtain was forty-five feet long and six feet wide. All eleven curtains had the same measurements. ¹⁶ He joined five of the curtains together, and the other six together. ¹⁷ He made fifty loops on the edge of the outermost curtain in the first set and fifty loops on the edge of the corresponding curtain in the second set. ¹⁸ He made fifty bronze clasps to join the tent together as a single unit. ¹⁹ He also made a covering for the tent from ram skins dyed red and a covering of fine leather on top of it.

²⁰ He made upright supports of acacia wood for the tabernacle. ²¹ Each support was fifteen feet long and twenty-seven inches wide. ²² Each support had two tenons for joining one to another. He did the same for all the supports of the tabernacle. ²³ He made supports for the tabernacle as follows: twenty for the south side, ²⁴ and he made forty silver bases to put under the twenty supports, two bases under the first support for its two tenons, and two bases under each of the following supports for their two tenons; ²⁵ for the second side of the tabernacle, the north side, he made twenty supports, ²⁶ with their forty silver bases, two bases under the first support and two bases under each of the following ones; ²⁷ and for the back of the tabernacle, on the west side, he made six supports. ²⁸ He also made two additional supports for the two back corners of the tabernacle. ²⁹ They were paired at the bottom and joined together at the top in a single ring. This is what he did with both of them for the two corners. ³⁰ So there were eight supports with their sixteen silver bases, two bases under each one.

³¹ He made five crossbars of acacia wood for the supports on one side of the tabernacle, ³² five crossbars for the supports on the other side of the tabernacle, and five crossbars for those at the back of the tabernacle on the west. ³³ He made the central crossbar run through the middle of the supports from one end to the other. ³⁴ He overlaid them with gold and made their rings out of gold as holders for the crossbars. He also overlaid the crossbars with gold.

³⁵ Then he made the curtain with blue, purple, and scarlet yarn, and finely spun linen. He made it with a design of cherubim worked into it. ³⁶ He made four pillars of acacia wood for it and overlaid them with gold; their hooks were of gold. And he cast four silver bases for the pillars.

³⁷ He made a screen embroidered with blue, purple, and scarlet yarn, and finely spun linen for the entrance to the tent, ³⁸ together with its five pillars and their hooks. He overlaid the tops of the pillars and their bands with gold, but their five bases were bronze.

CONTINUED

The materials were sufficient for them to do all the work. There was more than enough. EXODUS 36:7

The Tabernacle
and Courtyard

This portable temple, comprised of a tabernacle within a courtyard, was designed and built according to the instructions God gave Moses on Mount Sinai (Ex 25-31; 35-40). During their forty years in the wilderness, the Israelites would set up this tabernacle in the middle of their camp when they stopped. This was the place where the presence of the Lord would descend to meet with Moses and the priests (Ex 40:33-35).

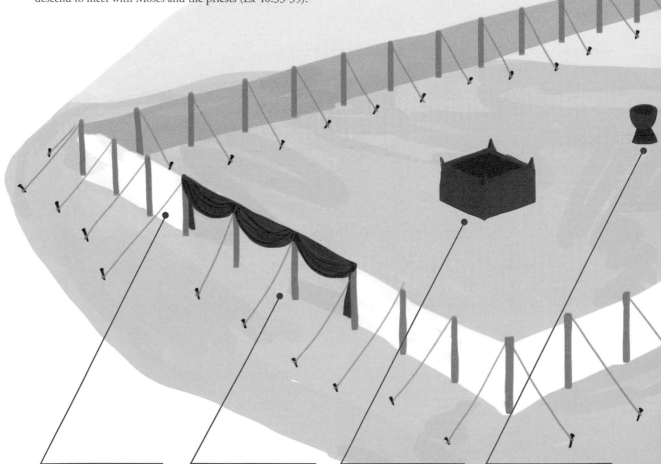

Courtyard Posts and Curtains

EX 27:9-19; 38:9-17

Made of finely spun linen and hung between sixty wooden posts with bronze bases and silver hooks. Formed a rectangular boundary around the 150-foot by 75-foot courtyard.

Courtyard Entrance

EX 38:18-20

Thirty feet by 7½-feet curtains made of finely spun linen embroidered with blue, purple, and scarlet yarn. Hung from silver hooks between four posts with bronze bases.

Bronze Altar

EX 27:1-8; 38:1-7

Wooden box overlaid with bronze, with horns at each top corner. Carried on two wooden poles threaded through bronze rings. Used for burnt offerings.

Bronze Basin

EX 30:17-21; 38:8

Made from women's bronze mirrors and placed on a bronze stand. Used for priests' ceremonial washing.

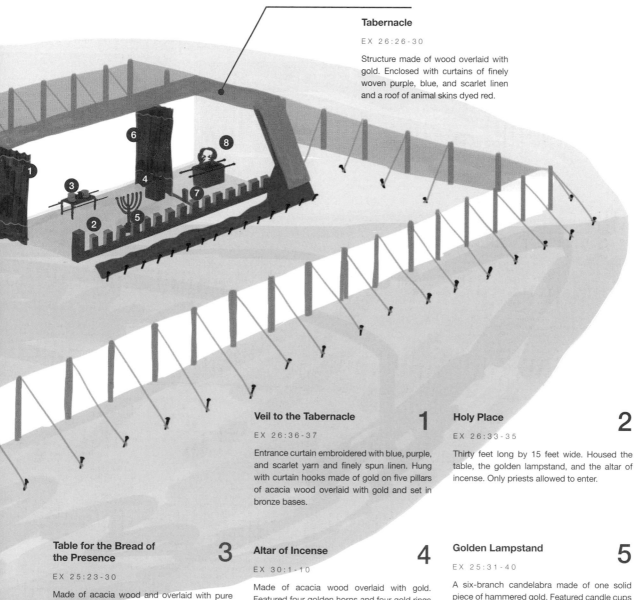

Tabernacle

EX 26:26-30

Structure made of wood overlaid with gold. Enclosed with curtains of finely woven purple, blue, and scarlet linen and a roof of animal skins dyed red.

Veil to the Tabernacle 1

EX 26:36-37

Entrance curtain embroidered with blue, purple, and scarlet yarn and finely spun linen. Hung with curtain hooks made of gold on five pillars of acacia wood overlaid with gold and set in bronze bases.

Holy Place 2

EX 26:33-35

Thirty feet long by 15 feet wide. Housed the table, the golden lampstand, and the altar of incense. Only priests allowed to enter.

Table for the Bread of the Presence 3

EX 25:23-30

Made of acacia wood and overlaid with pure gold, with a gold frame around its edge and gold rings attached to the legs for the carrying poles. Held a solid gold plate, pitcher, and cup for bread and drink offerings.

Altar of Incense 4

EX 30:1-10

Made of acacia wood overlaid with gold. Featured four golden horns and four gold rings for the carrying poles. Placed in front of the Most Holy Place. Used for burning the sacred incense.

Golden Lampstand 5

EX 25:31-40

A six-branch candelabra made of one solid piece of hammered gold. Featured candle cups shaped like almond blossoms. Used to illuminate the Holy Place.

Veil to the Most Holy Place 6

EX 26:31-33; 40:21

Screened the ark of the covenant from view (Ex 40:21). Made of blue, purple, and scarlet yarn and finely spun linen, with cherubim in the design. Only the high priest could pass through, once per year, to atone for Israel's sins (Heb 9:7).

Most Holy Place 7

EX 26:33-34

Where the Lord's presence would descend to meet with the priests. Housed only the ark of the covenant. Entered only once per year by the high priest, who brought the blood of atonement to the mercy seat.

Ark of the Covenant 8

EX 25:10-22

Made of acacia wood overlaid with pure gold. The lid was called the mercy seat, which featured two cherubim facing each other. Inside were the stone tablets from Sinai, and later a jar of manna and Aaron's staff that budded (Nm 17).

Matthew 27:50-51

[50] But Jesus cried out again with a loud voice and gave up his spirit. [51] Suddenly, the curtain of the sanctuary was torn in two from top to bottom, the earth quaked, and the rocks were split.

Hebrews 9:23-28

[23] Therefore, it was necessary for the copies of the things in the heavens to be purified with these sacrifices, but the heavenly things themselves to be purified with better sacrifices than these.

[24] For Christ did not enter a sanctuary made with hands (only a model of the true one) but into heaven itself,

so that he might now appear in the presence of God for us. [25] He did not do this to offer himself many times, as the high priest enters the sanctuary yearly with the blood of another. [26] Otherwise, he would have had to suffer many times since the foundation of the world. But now he has appeared one time, at the end of the ages, for the removal of sin by the sacrifice of himself. [27] And just as it is appointed for people to die once—and after this, judgment— [28] so also Christ, having been offered once to bear the sins of many, will appear a second time, not to bear sin, but to bring salvation to those who are waiting for him.

Month   Day

Day 37
Making the Ark

Exodus 37
Making the Ark

Bezalel made the ark of acacia wood, forty-five inches long, twenty-seven inches wide, and twenty-seven inches high. ² He overlaid it with pure gold inside and out and made a gold molding all around it. ³ He cast four gold rings for it, for its four feet, two rings on one side and two rings on the other side. ⁴ He made poles of acacia wood and overlaid them with gold. ⁵ He inserted the poles into the rings on the sides of the ark for carrying the ark.

⁶ He made a mercy seat of pure gold, forty-five inches long and twenty-seven inches wide. ⁷ He made two cherubim of gold; he made them of hammered work at the two ends of the mercy seat, ⁸ one cherub at one end and one cherub at the other end. At each end, he made a cherub of one piece with the mercy seat. ⁹ They had wings spread out. They faced each other and covered the mercy seat with their wings. The faces of the cherubim were looking toward the mercy seat.

Making the Table

¹⁰ He constructed the table of acacia wood, thirty-six inches long, eighteen inches wide, and twenty-seven inches high. ¹¹ He overlaid it with pure gold and made a gold molding all around it. ¹² He made a three-inch frame all around it and made a gold molding all around its frame. ¹³ He cast four gold rings for it and attached the rings to the four corners at its four legs. ¹⁴ The rings were next to the frame as holders for the poles to carry the table. ¹⁵ He made the poles for carrying the table from acacia wood and overlaid them with gold. ¹⁶ He also made the utensils that would be on the table out of pure gold: its plates and cups, as well as its bowls and pitchers for pouring drink offerings.

Making the Lampstand

¹⁷ Then he made the lampstand out of pure hammered gold. He made it all of one piece: its base and shaft, its ornamental cups, and its buds and petals. ¹⁸ Six branches extended from its sides, three branches of the lampstand from one side and three branches of the lampstand from the other side. ¹⁹ There were three cups shaped like almond blossoms, each with a bud and petals, on one branch, and three cups shaped like almond blossoms, each with a bud and petals, on the next branch. It was this way for the six branches that extended from the lampstand. ²⁰ There were four cups shaped like almond blossoms on the lampstand shaft along with its buds and petals. ²¹ For the six branches that extended from it, a bud was under the first pair of branches from it, a bud under the second pair of branches from it, and a bud under the third pair of branches from it. ²² Their buds and branches were of one piece with it. All of it was a single hammered piece of pure gold. ²³ He also made its seven lamps, snuffers, and firepans of pure gold. ²⁴ He made it and all its utensils of seventy-five pounds of pure gold.

Making the Altar of Incense

²⁵ He made the altar of incense out of acacia wood. It was square, eighteen inches long and eighteen inches wide; it was thirty-six inches high. Its horns were of one piece with it. ²⁶ He overlaid it, its top, all around its sides, and its horns with pure gold. Then he made a gold molding all around it. ²⁷ He made two gold rings for it under the molding on two of its sides; he put these on opposite sides of it to be holders for the poles to carry it with. ²⁸ He made the poles of acacia wood and overlaid them with gold.

²⁹ He also made the holy anointing oil and the pure, fragrant, and expertly blended incense.

Jeremiah 1:11-12
Two Visions

¹¹ Then the word of the LORD came to me, asking, "What do you see, Jeremiah?"

I replied, "I see a branch of an almond tree."

¹² The LORD said to me, "You have seen correctly, for I watch over my word to accomplish it."

Revelation 1:12-20

¹² Then I turned to see whose voice it was that spoke to me. When I turned I saw seven golden lampstands, ¹³ and among the lampstands was one like the Son of Man, dressed in a robe and with a golden sash wrapped around his chest. ¹⁴ The hair of his head was white as wool—white as snow—and his eyes like a fiery flame. ¹⁵ His feet were like fine bronze as it is fired in a furnace, and his voice like the sound of cascading waters. ¹⁶ He had seven stars in his right hand; a sharp double-edged sword came from his mouth, and his face was shining like the sun at full strength.

¹⁷ When I saw him, I fell at his feet like a dead man. He laid his right hand on me and said, "Don't be afraid.

I am the First and the Last,

¹⁸ and the Living One. I was dead, but look—I am alive forever and ever, and I hold the keys of death and Hades. ¹⁹ Therefore write what you have seen, what is, and what will take place after this. ²⁰ The mystery of the seven stars you saw in my right hand and of the seven golden lampstands is this: The seven stars are the angels of the seven churches, and the seven lampstands are the seven churches."

Day 38
Furnishing the Courtyard

Exodus 38
Making the Altar of Burnt Offering

Bezalel constructed the altar of burnt offering from acacia wood. It was square, 7½ feet long and 7½ feet wide, and was 4½ feet high. [2] He made horns for it on its four corners; the horns were of one piece with it. Then he overlaid it with bronze.

[3] He made all the altar's utensils: the pots, shovels, basins, meat forks, and firepans; he made all its utensils of bronze. [4] He constructed for the altar a grate of bronze mesh under its ledge, halfway up from the bottom. [5] He cast four rings at the four corners of the bronze grate as holders for the poles. [6] He made the poles of acacia wood and overlaid them with bronze. [7] Then he inserted the poles into the rings on the sides of the altar in order to carry it with them. He constructed the altar with boards so that it was hollow.

Making the Bronze Basin

[8] He made the bronze basin and its stand from the bronze mirrors of the women who served at the entrance to the tent of meeting.

Making the Courtyard

[9] Then he made the courtyard. The hangings on the south side of the courtyard were of finely spun linen, 150 feet long, [10] including their twenty posts and their twenty bronze bases, with silver hooks and silver bands for the posts. [11] The hangings on the north side were also 150 feet long, including their twenty posts and twenty bronze bases. The hooks and bands of the posts were silver. [12] The hangings on the west side were 75 feet long, including their ten posts and their ten bases, with silver hooks and silver bands for the posts. [13] And for the east side toward the sunrise, 75 feet long, [14] the hangings on one side of the gate were 22½ feet, including their three posts

and their three bases. ¹⁵ It was the same for the other side of the courtyard gate. The hangings were 22½ feet, including their three posts and their three bases. ¹⁶ All the hangings around the courtyard were of finely spun linen. ¹⁷ The bases for the posts were bronze; the hooks and bands of the posts were silver; and the plating for the tops of the posts was silver. All the posts of the courtyard were banded with silver.

¹⁸ The screen for the gate of the courtyard was made of finely spun linen, expertly embroidered with blue, purple, and scarlet yarn. It was 30 feet long, and like the hangings of the courtyard, 7½ feet high. ¹⁹ It had four posts with their four bronze bases. Their hooks were silver, and their top plating and their bands were silver. ²⁰ All the tent pegs for the tabernacle and for the surrounding courtyard were bronze.

Inventory of Materials

²¹ This is the inventory for the tabernacle, the tabernacle of the testimony, that was recorded at Moses's command. It was the work of the Levites under the direction of Ithamar son of Aaron the priest. ²² Bezalel son of Uri, son of Hur, of the tribe of Judah, made everything that the LORD commanded Moses. ²³ With him was Oholiab son of Ahisamach, of the tribe of Dan, a gem cutter, a designer, and an embroiderer with blue, purple, and scarlet yarn, and fine linen.

²⁴ All the gold of the presentation offering that was used for the project in all the work on the sanctuary, was 2,193 pounds, according to the sanctuary shekel. ²⁵ The silver from those of the community who were registered was 7,544 pounds, according to the sanctuary shekel— ²⁶ two-fifths of an ounce per man, that is, half a shekel according to the sanctuary shekel, from everyone twenty years old or more who had crossed over to the registered group, 603,550 men. ²⁷ There were 7,500 pounds of silver used to cast the bases of the sanctuary and the bases of the curtain—one hundred bases from 7,500 pounds, 75 pounds for each base. ²⁸ With the remaining 44 pounds he made the hooks for the posts, overlaid their tops, and supplied bands for them.

²⁹ The bronze of the presentation offering totaled 5,310 pounds. ³⁰ He made with it the bases for the entrance to the tent of meeting, the bronze altar and its bronze grate, all the utensils for the altar, ³¹ the bases for the surrounding courtyard, the bases for the gate of the courtyard, all the tent pegs for the tabernacle, and all the tent pegs for the surrounding courtyard.

Psalm 51:14-17

¹⁴ Save me from the guilt of bloodshed, God—
God of my salvation—
and my tongue will sing of your righteousness.

He made the bronze basin and its stand from the bronze mirrors of the women… EXODUS 38:8

¹⁵ Lord, open my lips,
and my mouth will declare your praise.
¹⁶ You do not want a sacrifice, or I would give it;
you are not pleased with a burnt offering.
¹⁷ The sacrifice pleasing to God is a broken spirit.
You will not despise a broken and humbled heart, God.

Hebrews 10:1-14
The Perfect Sacrifice

¹ Since the law has only a shadow of the good things to come, and not the reality itself of those things, it can never perfect the worshipers by the same sacrifices they continually offer year after year. ² Otherwise, wouldn't they have stopped being offered, since the worshipers, purified once and for all, would no longer have any consciousness of sins? ³ But in the sacrifices there is a reminder of sins year after year. ⁴ For it is impossible for the blood of bulls and goats to take away sins.

⁵ Therefore, as he was coming into the world, he said:

You did not desire sacrifice and offering,
but you prepared a body for me.
⁶ You did not delight
in whole burnt offerings and sin offerings.
⁷ Then I said, "See—
it is written about me
in the scroll—
I have come to do your will, O God."

⁸ After he says above, You did not desire or delight in sacrifices and offerings, whole burnt offerings and sin offerings (which are offered according to the law), ⁹ he then says, See, I have come to do your will. He takes away the first to establish the second.

¹⁰ By this will, we have been sanctified through the offering of the body of Jesus Christ once for all time.

¹¹ Every priest stands day after day ministering and offering the same sacrifices time after time, which can never take away sins. ¹² But this man, after offering one sacrifice for sins forever, sat down at the right hand of God. ¹³ He is now waiting until his enemies are made his footstool. ¹⁴ For by one offering he has perfected forever those who are sanctified.

_____   _____

Month   Day

Day 39
Making the Priestly Garments

Exodus 39
Making the Priestly Garments

They made specially woven garments for ministry in the sanctuary, and the holy garments for Aaron from the blue, purple, and scarlet yarn, just as the LORD had commanded Moses.

Making the Ephod

[2] Bezalel made the ephod of gold, of blue, purple, and scarlet yarn, and of finely spun linen. [3] They hammered out thin sheets of gold, and he cut threads from them to interweave with the blue, purple, and scarlet yarn, and the fine linen in a skillful design. [4] They made shoulder pieces for attaching it; it was joined together at its two edges. [5] The artistically woven waistband that was on the ephod was of one piece with the ephod, according to the same workmanship of gold, of blue, purple, and scarlet yarn, and of finely spun linen, just as the LORD had commanded Moses.

[6] Then they mounted the onyx stones surrounded with gold filigree settings, engraved with the names of Israel's sons as a gem cutter engraves a seal. [7] He fastened them on the shoulder pieces of the ephod as memorial stones for the Israelites, just as the LORD had commanded Moses.

Making the Breastpiece

[8] He also made the embroidered breastpiece with the same workmanship as the ephod of gold, of blue, purple, and scarlet yarn, and of finely spun linen. [9] They made the breastpiece square and folded double, nine inches long and nine inches wide. [10] They mounted four rows of gemstones on it.

The first row was

a row of carnelian, topaz, and emerald;

¹¹ the second row,

a turquoise, a lapis lazuli, and a diamond;

¹² the third row,

a jacinth, an agate, and an amethyst;

¹³ and the fourth row,

a beryl, an onyx, and a jasper.

They were surrounded with gold filigree in their settings.

¹⁴ The twelve stones corresponded to the names of Israel's sons. Each stone was engraved like a seal with one of the names of the twelve tribes.

¹⁵ They made braided chains of pure gold cord for the breastpiece. ¹⁶ They also fashioned two gold filigree settings and two gold rings and attached the two rings to its two corners. ¹⁷ Then they attached the two gold cords to the two gold rings on the corners of the breastpiece. ¹⁸ They attached the other ends of the two cords to the two filigree settings, and in this way they attached them to the ephod's shoulder pieces in front. ¹⁹ They made two other gold rings and put them at the two other corners of the breastpiece on the edge that is next to the inner border of the ephod. ²⁰ They made two more gold rings and attached them to the bottom of the ephod's two shoulder pieces on its front, close to its seam, above the ephod's woven waistband. ²¹ Then they tied the breastpiece from its rings to the rings of the ephod with a cord of blue yarn, so that the breastpiece was above the ephod's waistband and did not come loose from the ephod. They did just as the LORD had commanded Moses.

Making the Robe

²² They made the woven robe of the ephod entirely of blue yarn. ²³ There was an opening in the center of the robe like that of body armor with a collar around the opening so that it would not tear. ²⁴ They made pomegranates of finely spun blue, purple, and scarlet yarn on the lower hem of the

robe. ²⁵ They made bells of pure gold and attached the bells between the pomegranates, all around the hem of the robe between the pomegranates, ²⁶ a bell and a pomegranate alternating all around the lower hem of the robe to be worn for ministry. They made it just as the LORD had commanded Moses.

The Other Priestly Garments

²⁷ They made the tunics of fine woven linen for Aaron and his sons. ²⁸ They made the turban and the ornate headbands of fine linen, the linen undergarments of finely spun linen, ²⁹ and the sash of finely spun linen expertly embroidered with blue, purple, and scarlet yarn. They did just as the LORD had commanded Moses.

Making the Holy Diadem

³⁰ They made a medallion, the holy diadem, out of pure gold and wrote on it an inscription like the engraving on a seal: HOLY TO THE LORD. ³¹ They attached a cord of blue yarn to it in order to mount it on the turban, just as the LORD had commanded Moses.

Moses's Inspection of the Tabernacle

³² So all the work for the tabernacle, the tent of meeting, was finished. The Israelites did everything just as the LORD had commanded Moses. ³³ They brought the tabernacle to Moses: the tent with all its furnishings, its clasps, its supports, its crossbars, and its pillars and bases; ³⁴ the covering of ram skins dyed red and the covering of fine leather; the curtain for the screen; ³⁵ the ark of the testimony with its poles and the mercy seat; ³⁶ the table, all its utensils, and the Bread of the Presence; ³⁷ the pure gold lampstand, with its lamps arranged and all its utensils, as well as the oil for the light; ³⁸ the gold altar; the anointing oil; the fragrant incense; the screen for the entrance to the tent; ³⁹ the bronze altar with its bronze grate, its poles, and all its utensils; the basin with its stand; ⁴⁰ the hangings of the courtyard, its posts and bases, the screen for the gate of the courtyard, its ropes and tent pegs, and all the furnishings for the service of the tabernacle,

They did just as the Lord had commanded Moses.

the tent of meeting; [41] and the specially woven garments for ministering in the sanctuary, the holy garments for the priest Aaron and the garments for his sons to serve as priests. [42] The Israelites had done all the work according to everything the Lord had commanded Moses. [43] Moses inspected all the work they had accomplished. They had done just as the Lord commanded. Then Moses blessed them.

Psalm 110
The Priestly King
A psalm of David.

[1] This is the declaration of the Lord
to my Lord:
"Sit at my right hand
until I make your enemies your footstool."
[2] The Lord will extend your mighty scepter from Zion.
Rule over your surrounding enemies.
[3] Your people will volunteer
on your day of battle.
In holy splendor, from the womb of the dawn,
the dew of your youth belongs to you.
[4] The Lord has sworn an oath and will not take it back:
"You are a priest forever
according to the pattern of Melchizedek."

Hebrews 5:1-10
Christ, a High Priest

[1] For every high priest taken from among men is appointed in matters pertaining to God for the people, to offer both gifts and sacrifices for sins. [2] He is able to deal gently with those who are ignorant and are going astray, since he is also clothed with weakness. [3] Because of this, he must make an offering for his own sins as well as for the people. [4] No one takes this honor on himself; instead, a person is called by God, just as Aaron was. [5] In the same way, Christ did not exalt himself to become a high priest, but God who said to him,

You are my Son;
today I have become your Father,

[6] also says in another place,

You are a priest forever
according to the order of Melchizedek.

[7] During his earthly life, he offered prayers and appeals with loud cries and tears to the one who was able to save him from death, and he was heard because of his reverence. [8] Although he was the Son, he learned obedience from what he suffered. [9] After he was perfected, he became the source of eternal salvation for all who obey him, [10] and he was declared by God a high priest according to the order of Melchizedek.

_____ _____
Month   Day

Notes

Day 40
The Glory of the Lord
Fills the Tabernacle

Exodus 40
Setting up the Tabernacle

The LORD spoke to Moses: ² "You are to set up the tabernacle, the tent of meeting, on the first day of the first month. ³ Put the ark of the testimony there and screen off the ark with the curtain. ⁴ Then bring in the table and lay out its arrangement; also bring in the lampstand and set up its lamps. ⁵ Place the gold altar for incense in front of the ark of the testimony. Put up the screen for the entrance to the tabernacle. ⁶ Position the altar of burnt offering in front of the entrance to the tabernacle, the tent of meeting. ⁷ Place the basin between the tent of meeting and the altar, and put water in it. ⁸ Assemble the surrounding courtyard and hang the screen for the gate of the courtyard.

⁹ "Take the anointing oil and anoint the tabernacle and everything in it; consecrate it along with all its furnishings so that it will be holy. ¹⁰ Anoint the altar of burnt offering and all its utensils; consecrate the altar so that it will be especially holy. ¹¹ Anoint the basin and its stand and consecrate it.

¹² "Then bring Aaron and his sons to the entrance to the tent of meeting and wash them with water. ¹³ Clothe Aaron with the holy garments, anoint him, and consecrate him, so that he can serve me as a priest. ¹⁴ Have his sons come forward and clothe them in tunics. ¹⁵ Anoint them just as you anointed their father, so that they may also serve me as priests. Their anointing will serve to inaugurate a permanent priesthood for them throughout their generations."

¹⁶ Moses did everything just as the LORD had commanded him. ¹⁷ The tabernacle was set up in the first month of the second year, on the first day of the month. ¹⁸ Moses set up the tabernacle: He laid its bases, positioned its supports, inserted its crossbars, and set up its pillars. ¹⁹ Then he spread the tent over the tabernacle and put the covering of the tent on top of it, just as the LORD had commanded Moses.

²⁰ Moses took the testimony and placed it in the ark, and attached the poles to the ark. He set the mercy seat on top of the ark. ²¹ He brought the ark into the tabernacle, put up the curtain for the screen, and screened off the ark of the testimony, just as the LORD had commanded him.

²² Moses placed the table in the tent of meeting on the north side of the tabernacle, outside the curtain. ²³ He arranged the bread on it before the LORD, just as the LORD had commanded him. ²⁴ He put the lampstand in the tent of meeting opposite the table on the south side of the tabernacle ²⁵ and set up the lamps before the LORD, just as the LORD had commanded him.

²⁶ Moses installed the gold altar in the tent of meeting, in front of the curtain, ²⁷ and burned fragrant incense on it, just as the LORD had commanded him. ²⁸ He put up the screen at the entrance to the tabernacle. ²⁹ He placed the altar of burnt offering at the entrance to the tabernacle, the tent of meeting, and offered the burnt offering and the grain offering on it, just as the LORD had commanded him.

³⁰ He set the basin between the tent of meeting and the altar and put water in it for washing. ³¹ Moses, Aaron, and his sons washed their hands and feet from it. ³² They washed whenever they came to the tent of meeting and approached the altar, just as the LORD had commanded Moses.

³³ Next Moses set up the surrounding courtyard for the tabernacle and the altar and hung a screen for the gate of the courtyard. So Moses finished the work.

The Lord's Glory

³⁴ The cloud covered the tent of meeting, and the glory of the LORD filled the tabernacle. ³⁵ Moses was unable to enter the tent of meeting because the cloud rested on it, and the glory of the LORD filled the tabernacle.

³⁶ The Israelites set out whenever the cloud was taken up from the tabernacle throughout all the stages of their journey. ³⁷ If the cloud was not taken up, they did not set out until the day it was taken up. ³⁸ For the cloud of the LORD was over the tabernacle by day, and there was a fire inside the cloud by night, visible to the entire house of Israel throughout all the stages of their journey.

The glory of the LORD filled the tabernacle. EXODUS 40:34

Matthew 3:16-17

[16] When Jesus was baptized, he went up immediately from the water. The heavens suddenly opened for him, and he saw the Spirit of God descending like a dove and coming down on him. [17] And a voice from heaven said: "This is my beloved Son, with whom I am well-pleased."

Acts 2:1-4

Pentecost

[1] When the day of Pentecost had arrived, they were all together in one place. [2] Suddenly a sound like that of a violent rushing wind came from heaven, and it filled the whole house where they were staying. [3] They saw tongues like flames of fire that separated and rested on each one of them. [4] Then they were all filled with the Holy Spirit and began to speak in different tongues, as the Spirit enabled them.

Notes

Day 41
Grace Day

Use today to pray, rest, and reflect on this week's reading, giving thanks for the grace that is ours in Christ.

You do not want a sacrifice, or I would give it;
you are not pleased with a burnt offering.
The sacrifice pleasing to God is a broken spirit.
You will not despise a broken and humbled heart, God.

PSALM 51:16-17

Morning Skillet

TOTAL TIME: 60 MINUTES

SERVES: 8

INGREDIENTS

6 eggs, beaten

2 cups sharp cheddar cheese, shredded

1 4-ounce can green chilis

¾ cup onion, chopped

½ teaspoon salt

Hot sauce, to taste

Rosemary, for garnish

DIRECTIONS

Preheat oven to 350°F.

Combine all ingredients in a mixing bowl.

Pour into a buttered and preheated 8-inch cast iron skillet or 9x9 glass baking dish, and bake 50-55 minutes.

Remove from oven and garnish with rosemary.

Section 3
See the Lord's Salvation

Holy Week

Exodus tells the story of the deliverance of God's people from oppression and tyranny into the freedom of His presence. Easter tells this same story on a much grander scale. The following readings walk through Jesus' final days, His crucifixion, and His resurrection. They tell how God has delivered us from our slavery to sin and brings us into glorious freedom as His children.

Jesus in the Book of Exodus

"Then beginning with Moses and all the Prophets, he interpreted for them the things concerning himself in all the Scriptures." – Luke 24:27

When Jesus talked about the Old Testament, He spoke of how it all points to Him. Here are some places where we see Jesus in Exodus.

"I AM"

EXODUS 3:1-6

When Moses asked the Lord for His name at the burning bush, God replied, "I AM."

Jesus uses "I AM" to refer to His divinity both metaphorically (Jn 6:35, 48, 51; 8:12; 9:5; 10:7-14; 11:25; 14:6; 15:1) and directly (Jn 6:20; 8:24, 28, 58; 18:5).

The Passover Lamb

EXODUS 12:1-28

An unblemished lamb was slain to spare the lives of the firstborn sons during the tenth plague.

We have been redeemed "with the precious blood of Christ, like that of an unblemished and spotless lamb" (1Pt 1:19). "Christ our Passover lamb has been sacrificed" for us (1Co 5:7).

Bread from Heaven

EXODUS 16

Daily bread came down from heaven to sustain the Israelites in the desert.

Jesus said, "I am the bread of life. No one who comes to me will ever be hungry" (Jn 6:35).

The Rock Flowing with Living Water

The Tabernacle

The Priest

EXODUS 17:1-7

Miraculous water flowed from a rock in the desert, keeping the Israelites alive.

EXODUS 36-39

The tent in the middle of the camp where the glorious presence of the Lord dwelled.

EXODUS 40:12-15

Priests were ceremonially holy and set apart to represent the Israelites before God, offering sacrifices to atone for their sin.

"That rock was Christ" (1Co 10:4). Jesus said, "Whoever drinks from the water that I will give him will never get thirsty again. In fact, the water I will give him will become a well of water springing up in him for eternal life" (Jn 4:13-14).

"The Word became flesh and dwelt among us. We observed his glory, the glory as the one and only Son from the Father, full of grace and truth" (Jn 1:14).

Jesus is "the kind of high priest we need: holy, innocent, undefiled, separated from sinners, and exalted above the heavens" (Heb 7:26).

Day 42
Palm Sunday

Luke 19:28-44
The Triumphal Entry

²⁸ When he had said these things, he went on ahead, going up to Jerusalem. ²⁹ As he approached Bethphage and Bethany, at the place called the Mount of Olives, he sent two of the disciples ³⁰ and said, "Go into the village ahead of you. As you enter it, you will find a young donkey tied there, on which no one has ever sat. Untie it and bring it. ³¹ If anyone asks you, 'Why are you untying it?' say this: 'The Lord needs it.'"

³² So those who were sent left and found it just as he had told them. ³³ As they were untying the young donkey, its owners said to them, "Why are you untying the donkey?"

³⁴ "The Lord needs it," they said. ³⁵ Then they brought it to Jesus, and after throwing their clothes on the donkey, they helped Jesus get on it. ³⁶ As he was going along, they were spreading their clothes on the road. ³⁷ Now he came near the path down the Mount of Olives, and the whole crowd of the disciples began to praise God joyfully with a loud voice for all the miracles they had seen:

> ³⁸ Blessed is the King who comes
> in the name of the Lord.
> Peace in heaven
> and glory in the highest heaven!

³⁹ Some of the Pharisees from the crowd told him, "Teacher, rebuke your disciples."

⁴⁰ He answered, "I tell you, if they were to keep silent, the stones would cry out."

Jesus's Love for Jerusalem

⁴¹ As he approached and saw the city, he wept for it, ⁴² saying, "If you knew this day what would bring peace—but now it is hidden from your eyes. ⁴³ For the days will come on you when your enemies will build a barricade around you, surround you, and hem you in on every side. ⁴⁴ They will crush you and your children among you to the ground, and they will not leave one stone on another in your midst, because you did not recognize the time when God visited you."

Zechariah 9:9
The Coming of Zion's King

> Rejoice greatly, Daughter Zion!
> Shout in triumph, Daughter Jerusalem!
> Look, your King is coming to you;
> he is righteous and victorious,
> humble and riding on a donkey,
> on a colt, the foal of a donkey.

Psalm 118:25-29

> ²⁵ Lᴏʀᴅ, save us!
> Lᴏʀᴅ, please grant us success!
> ²⁶ He who comes in the name
> of the Lᴏʀᴅ is blessed.
> From the house of the Lᴏʀᴅ we bless you.
> ²⁷ The Lᴏʀᴅ is God and has given us light.
> Bind the festival sacrifice with cords
> to the horns of the altar.
> ²⁸ You are my God, and I will give you thanks.
> You are my God; I will exalt you.
> ²⁹ Give thanks to the Lᴏʀᴅ, for he is good;
> his faithful love endures forever.

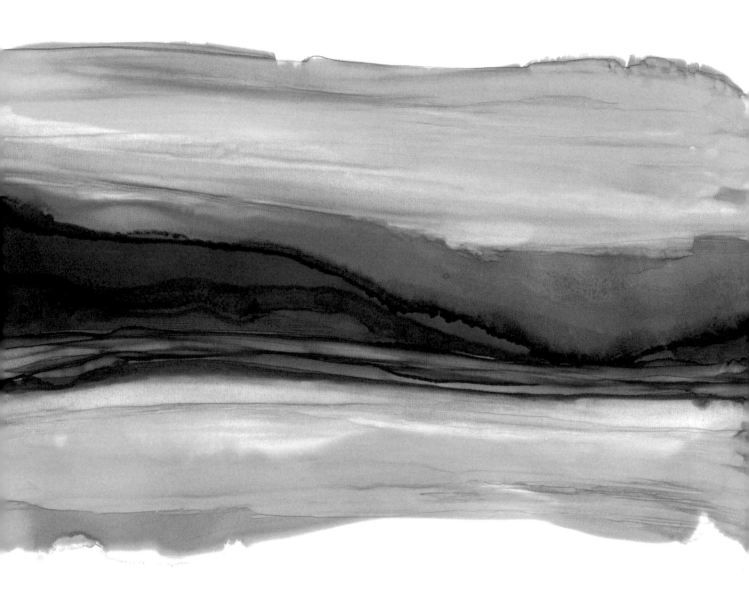

NOTES

Day 43
Jesus Cleanses the Temple

Mark 11:12-19

The Barren Fig Tree Is Cursed

[12] The next day when they went out from Bethany, he was hungry. [13] Seeing in the distance a fig tree with leaves, he went to find out if there was anything on it. When he came to it, he found nothing but leaves; for it was not the season for figs. [14] He said to it, "May no one ever eat fruit from you again!" And his disciples heard it.

Cleansing the Temple

[15] They came to Jerusalem, and he went into the temple and began to throw out those buying and selling. He overturned the tables of the money changers and the chairs of those selling doves, [16] and would not permit anyone to carry goods through the temple. [17] He was teaching them:

"Is it not written, My house will be called a house of prayer for all nations? But you have made it a den of thieves!"

[18] The chief priests and the scribes heard it and started looking for a way to kill him. For they were afraid of him, because the whole crowd was astonished by his teaching.

[19] Whenever evening came, they would go out of the city.

Isaiah 56:1-8
A House of Prayer for All

¹ This is what the Lord says:

Preserve justice and do what is right,
for my salvation is coming soon,
and my righteousness will be revealed.
² Happy is the person who does this,
the son of man who holds it fast,
who keeps the Sabbath without desecrating it,
and keeps his hand from doing any evil.

³ No foreigner who has joined himself to the Lord
should say,
"The Lord will exclude me from his people,"
and the eunuch should not say,
"Look, I am a dried-up tree."
⁴ For the Lord says this:
"For the eunuchs who keep my Sabbaths,
and choose what pleases me,
and hold firmly to my covenant,
⁵ I will give them, in my house and within my walls,
a memorial and a name
better than sons and daughters.
I will give each of them an everlasting name
that will never be cut off.
⁶ As for the foreigners who join themselves to the Lord
to minister to him, to love the name of the Lord,
and to become his servants—
all who keep the Sabbath without desecrating it
and who hold firmly to my covenant—
⁷ I will bring them to my holy mountain
and let them rejoice in my house of prayer.
Their burnt offerings and sacrifices
will be acceptable on my altar,
for my house will be called a house of prayer
for all nations."
⁸ This is the declaration of the Lord God,
who gathers the dispersed of Israel:
"I will gather to them still others
besides those already gathered."

NOTES

Wk.**7**

Day 44
Jesus Teaches in the Temple

Luke 21
The Widow's Gift

¹ He looked up and saw the rich dropping their offerings into the temple treasury. ² He also saw a poor widow dropping in two tiny coins. ³ "Truly I tell you," he said. "This poor widow has put in more than all of them. ⁴ For all these people have put in gifts out of their surplus, but she out of her poverty has put in all she had to live on."

Destruction of the Temple Predicted

⁵ As some were talking about the temple, how it was adorned with beautiful stones and gifts dedicated to God, he said, ⁶ "These things that you see—the days will come when not one stone will be left on another that will not be thrown down."

Signs of the End of the Age

⁷ "Teacher," they asked him, "so when will these things happen? And what will be the sign when these things are about to take place?"

⁸ Then he said,

"Watch out that you are not deceived.

For many will come in my name, saying, 'I am he,' and, 'The time is near.' Don't follow them. ⁹ When you hear of wars and rebellions, don't be alarmed. Indeed, it is necessary that these things take place first, but the end won't come right away."

¹⁰ Then he told them: "Nation will be raised up against nation, and kingdom against kingdom. ¹¹ There will be violent earthquakes, and famines and plagues in various places, and there will be terrifying sights and great signs from heaven. ¹² But before all these things, they will lay their hands on you and persecute you. They will hand you over to the synagogues and prisons, and you will be brought before kings and governors because of my name. ¹³ This will give you an opportunity to bear witness. ¹⁴ Therefore make up your minds not to prepare your defense ahead of time, ¹⁵ for I will give you such words and a wisdom that none of your adversaries will be able to resist or contradict. ¹⁶ You will even be betrayed by parents, brothers, relatives, and friends. They will kill some of you. ¹⁷ You will be hated by everyone because of my name, ¹⁸ but not a hair of your head will be lost. ¹⁹ By your endurance, gain your lives.

The Destruction of Jerusalem

²⁰ "When you see Jerusalem surrounded by armies, then recognize that its desolation has come near. ²¹ Then those in Judea must flee to the mountains. Those inside the city must leave it, and those who are in the country must not enter it, ²² because these are days of vengeance to fulfill all the things that are written. ²³ Woe to pregnant women and nursing mothers in those days, for there will be great distress in the land and wrath against this people. ²⁴ They will be killed by the sword and be led captive into all the nations, and Jerusalem will be trampled by the Gentiles until the times of the Gentiles are fulfilled.

The Coming of the Son of Man

²⁵ "Then there will be signs in the sun, moon, and stars; and there will be anguish on the earth among nations bewildered by the roaring of the sea and the waves. ²⁶ People will faint from fear and expectation of the things that are coming on the world, because the powers of the heavens will be shaken. ²⁷ Then they will see the Son of Man coming in a cloud with power and great glory. ²⁸ But when these things begin to take place, stand up and lift up your heads, because your redemption is near."

The Parable of the Fig Tree

²⁹ Then he told them a parable: "Look at the fig tree, and all the trees. ³⁰ As soon as they put out leaves you can see

for yourselves and recognize that summer is already near. [31] In the same way, when you see these things happening, recognize that the kingdom of God is near. [32] Truly I tell you, this generation will certainly not pass away until all things take place. [33] Heaven and earth will pass away, but my words will never pass away.

The Need for Watchfulness

[34] "Be on your guard, so that your minds are not dulled from carousing, drunkenness, and worries of life, or that day will come on you unexpectedly [35] like a trap. For it will come on all who live on the face of the whole earth. [36] But be alert at all times, praying that you may have strength to escape all these things that are going to take place and to stand before the Son of Man."

[37] During the day, he was teaching in the temple, but in the evening he would go out and spend the night on what is called the Mount of Olives. [38] Then all the people would come early in the morning to hear him in the temple.

Luke 22:1-2
The Plot to Kill Jesus

[1] The Festival of Unleavened Bread, which is called Passover, was approaching. [2] The chief priests and the scribes were looking for a way to put him to death, because they were afraid of the people.

Daniel 7:13-14

[13] I continued watching in the night visions,

and suddenly one like a son of man
was coming with the clouds of heaven.
He approached the Ancient of Days
and was escorted before him.
[14] He was given dominion,
and glory, and a kingdom;
so that those of every people,
nation, and language
should serve him.
His dominion is an everlasting dominion that will not pass
away, and his kingdom is one that will not be destroyed.

"Heaven and earth will pass away, but my words will never pass away." LUKE 21:33

Day 45
Jesus Is Anointed for Burial

Mark 14:3-11
The Anointing at Bethany

[3] While he was in Bethany at the house of Simon the leper, as he was reclining at the table, a woman came with an alabaster jar of very expensive perfume of pure nard. She broke the jar and poured it on his head. [4] But some were expressing indignation to one another: "Why has this perfume been wasted? [5] For this perfume might have been sold for more than three hundred denarii and given to the poor." And they began to scold her.

[6] Jesus replied, "Leave her alone. Why are you bothering her? She has done a noble thing for me. [7] You always have the poor with you, and you can do what is good for them whenever you want, but you do not always have me. [8] She has done what she could; she has anointed my body in advance for burial.

[9] Truly I tell you, wherever the gospel is proclaimed in the whole world, what she has done will also be told in memory of her."

[10] Then Judas Iscariot, one of the Twelve, went to the chief priests to betray Jesus to them. [11] And when they heard this, they were glad and promised to give him money. So he started looking for a good opportunity to betray him.

Matthew 26:14-16

[14] Then one of the Twelve, the man called Judas Iscariot, went to the chief priests [15] and said, "What are you willing to give me if I hand him over to you?" So they weighed out thirty pieces of silver for him. [16] And from that time he started looking for a good opportunity to betray him.

Luke 22:3-6

3 Then Satan entered Judas, called Iscariot, who was numbered among the Twelve. 4 He went away and discussed with the chief priests and temple police how he could hand him over to them. 5 They were glad and agreed to give him silver. 6 So he accepted the offer and started looking for a good opportunity to betray him to them when the crowd was not present.

Zechariah 11:12-13

12 Then I said to them, "If it seems right to you, give me my wages; but if not, keep them." So they weighed my wages, thirty pieces of silver.

13 "Throw it to the potter," the Lord said to me—this magnificent price I was valued by them. So I took the thirty pieces of silver and threw it into the house of the Lord, to the potter.

"She has done a noble thing for me." MARK 14:6

Day 46
The Last Supper

John 16:16-24, 32-33
Sorrow Turned to Joy

¹⁶ "A little while and you will no longer see me; again a little while and you will see me."

¹⁷ Then some of his disciples said to one another, "What is this he's telling us: 'A little while and you will not see me; again a little while and you will see me' and, 'because I am going to the Father'?" ¹⁸ They said, "What is this he is saying, 'A little while'? We don't know what he's talking about."

¹⁹ Jesus knew they wanted to ask him, and so he said to them, "Are you asking one another about what I said, 'A little while and you will not see me; again a little while and you will see me'? ²⁰ Truly I tell you, you will weep and mourn, but the world will rejoice.

You will become sorrowful, but your sorrow will turn to joy.

²¹ When a woman is in labor, she has pain because her time has come. But when she has given birth to a child, she no longer remembers the suffering because of the joy that a person has been born into the world. ²² So you also have sorrow now. But I will see you again. Your hearts will rejoice, and no one will take away your joy from you.

²³ "In that day you will not ask me anything. Truly I tell you, anything you ask the Father in my name, he will give you. ²⁴ Until now you have asked for nothing in my name. Ask and you will receive, so that your joy may be complete."

…

[32] "Indeed, an hour is coming, and has come, when each of you will be scattered to his own home, and you will leave me alone. Yet I am not alone, because the Father is with me. [33] I have told you these things so that in me you may have peace. You will have suffering in this world. Be courageous! I have conquered the world."

Mark 14:12-72

Preparation for Passover

[12] On the first day of Unleavened Bread, when they sacrifice the Passover lamb, his disciples asked him, "Where do you want us to go and prepare the Passover so that you may eat it?"

[13] So he sent two of his disciples and told them, "Go into the city, and a man carrying a jar of water will meet you. Follow him. [14] Wherever he enters, tell the owner of the house, 'The Teacher says, "Where is my guest room where I may eat the Passover with my disciples?"' [15] He will show you a large room upstairs, furnished and ready. Make the preparations for us there." [16] So the disciples went out, entered the city, and found it just as he had told them, and they prepared the Passover.

Betrayal at the Passover

[17] When evening came, he arrived with the Twelve. [18] While they were reclining and eating, Jesus said, "Truly I tell you, one of you will betray me—one who is eating with me."

[19] They began to be distressed and to say to him one by one, "Surely not I?"

[20] He said to them, "It is one of the Twelve—the one who is dipping bread in the bowl with me. [21] For the Son of Man will go just as it is written about him, but woe to that man by whom the Son of Man is betrayed! It would have been better for him if he had not been born."

The First Lord's Supper

[22] As they were eating, he took bread, blessed and broke it, gave it to them, and said,

"Take it; this is my body."

[23] Then he took a cup, and after giving thanks, he gave it to them, and they all drank from it. [24] He said to them, "This is my blood of the covenant, which is poured out for many. [25] Truly I tell you, I will no longer drink of the fruit of the vine until that day when I drink it new in the kingdom of God."

[26] After singing a hymn, they went out to the Mount of Olives.

"Take it; this is my body." MARK 14:22

Peter's Denial Predicted

²⁷ Then Jesus said to them, "All of you will fall away, because it is written:

> I will strike the shepherd,
> and the sheep will be scattered.

²⁸ But after I have risen, I will go ahead of you to Galilee."

²⁹ Peter told him, "Even if everyone falls away, I will not."

³⁰ "Truly I tell you," Jesus said to him, "today, this very night, before the rooster crows twice, you will deny me three times."

³¹ But he kept insisting, "If I have to die with you, I will never deny you." And they all said the same thing.

The Prayer in the Garden

³² Then they came to a place named Gethsemane, and he told his disciples, "Sit here while I pray." ³³ He took Peter, James, and John with him, and he began to be deeply distressed and troubled. ³⁴ He said to them, "I am deeply grieved to the point of death. Remain here and stay awake." ³⁵ He went a little farther, fell to the ground, and prayed that if it were possible, the hour might pass from him. ³⁶ And he said,

"Abba, Father! All things are possible for you. Take this cup away from me. Nevertheless, not what I will, but what you will."

³⁷ Then he came and found them sleeping. He said to Peter, "Simon, are you sleeping? Couldn't you stay awake one hour? ³⁸ Stay awake and pray so that you won't enter into temptation. The spirit is willing, but the flesh is weak." ³⁹ Once again he went away and prayed, saying the same thing. ⁴⁰ And again he came and found them sleeping, because they could not keep their eyes open. They did not know what to say to him. ⁴¹ Then he came a third time and said to them, "Are you still sleeping and resting? Enough! The time has come. See, the Son of Man is betrayed into the hands of sinners. ⁴² Get up; let's go. See, my betrayer is near."

CONTINUED

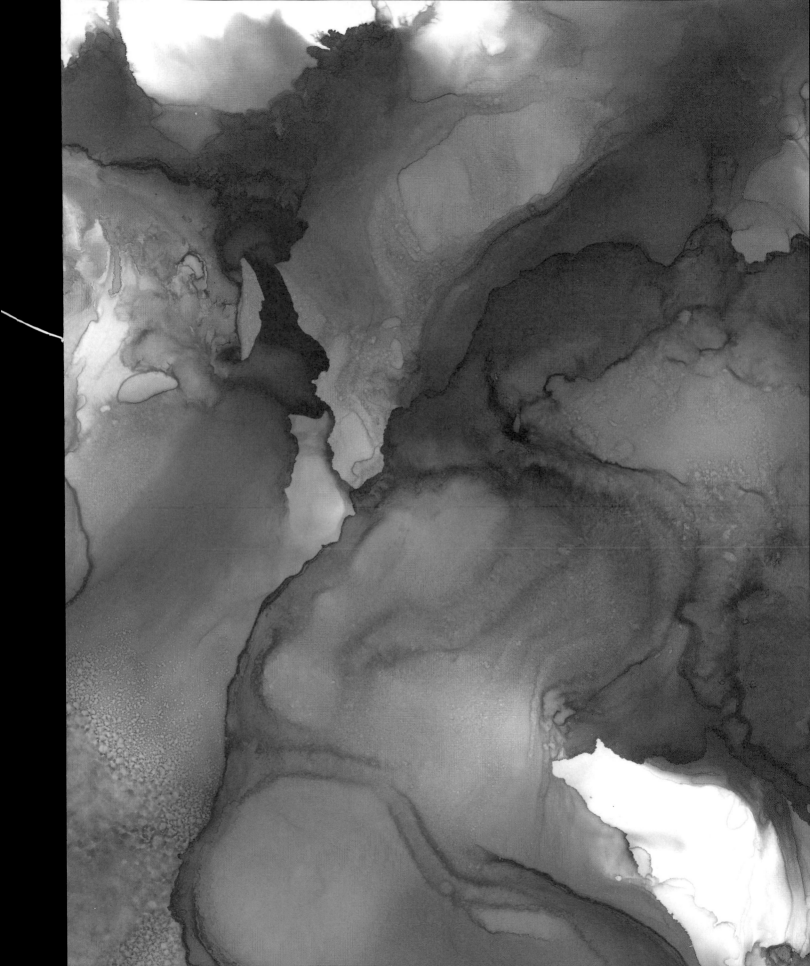

Judas's Betrayal of Jesus

43 While he was still speaking, Judas, one of the Twelve, suddenly arrived. With him was a mob, with swords and clubs, from the chief priests, the scribes, and the elders. 44 His betrayer had given them a signal. "The one I kiss," he said, "he's the one; arrest him and take him away under guard." 45 So when he came, immediately he went up to Jesus and said, "Rabbi!" and kissed him. 46 They took hold of him and arrested him. 47 One of those who stood by drew his sword, struck the high priest's servant, and cut off his ear.

48 Jesus said to them, "Have you come out with swords and clubs, as if I were a criminal, to capture me? 49 Every day I was among you, teaching in the temple, and you didn't arrest me. But the Scriptures must be fulfilled."

50 Then they all deserted him and ran away. 51 Now a certain young man, wearing nothing but a linen cloth, was following him. They caught hold of him, 52 but he left the linen cloth behind and ran away naked.

Jesus Faces the Sanhedrin

53 They led Jesus away to the high priest, and all the chief priests, the elders, and the scribes assembled. 54 Peter followed him at a distance, right into the high priest's courtyard. He was sitting with the servants, warming himself by the fire.

55 The chief priests and the whole Sanhedrin were looking for testimony against Jesus to put him to death, but they could not find any. 56 For many were giving false testimony against him, and the testimonies did not agree. 57 Some stood up and gave false testimony against him, stating, 58 "We heard him say, 'I will destroy this temple made with human hands, and in three days I will build another not made by hands.'" 59 Yet their testimony did not agree even on this.

60 Then the high priest stood up before them all and questioned Jesus, "Don't you have an answer to what these men are testifying against you?" 61 But he kept silent and did not answer. Again the high priest questioned him, "Are you the Messiah, the Son of the Blessed One?"

62 "I am," said Jesus, "and you will see the Son of Man seated at the right hand of Power and coming with the clouds of heaven."

63 Then the high priest tore his robes and said, "Why do we still need witnesses? 64 You have heard the blasphemy. What is your decision?" They all condemned him as deserving death.

65 Then some began to spit on him, to blindfold him, and to beat him, saying, "Prophesy!" The temple servants also took him and slapped him.

Peter Denies His Lord

66 While Peter was in the courtyard below, one of the high priest's maidservants came. 67 When she saw Peter warming himself, she looked at him and said, "You also were with Jesus, the man from Nazareth."

68 But he denied it: "I don't know or understand what you're talking about." Then he went out to the entryway, and a rooster crowed.

69 When the maidservant saw him again, she began to tell those standing nearby, "This man is one of them."

70 But again he denied it. After a little while those standing there said to Peter again, "You certainly are one of them, since you're also a Galilean."

71 Then he started to curse and swear, "I don't know this man you're talking about!"

72 Immediately a rooster crowed a second time, and Peter remembered when Jesus had spoken the word to him, "Before the rooster crows twice, you will deny me three times." And he broke down and wept.

Psalm 41:7-13

7 All who hate me whisper together about me;
they plan to harm me.
8 "Something awful has overwhelmed him,
and he won't rise again from where he lies!"
9 Even my friend in whom I trusted,
one who ate my bread,
has raised his heel against me.

10 But you, LORD, be gracious to me and raise me up;
then I will repay them.
11 By this I know that you delight in me:
my enemy does not shout in triumph over me.
12 You supported me because of my integrity
and set me in your presence forever.

13 Blessed be the LORD God of Israel,
from everlasting to everlasting.
Amen and amen.

Zechariah 13:7

Sword, awake against my shepherd,
against the man who is my associate—
this is the declaration of the LORD of Armies.
Strike the shepherd, and the sheep will be scattered;
I will turn my hand against the little ones.

Wk.**7**

Day 47
Good Friday

Mark 15
Jesus Faces Pilate

[1] As soon as it was morning, having held a meeting with the elders, scribes, and the whole Sanhedrin, the chief priests tied Jesus up, led him away, and handed him over to Pilate.

[2] So Pilate asked him, "Are you the King of the Jews?"

He answered him,

"You say so."

[3] And the chief priests accused him of many things. [4] Pilate questioned him again, "Aren't you going to answer? Look how many things they are accusing you of!" [5] But Jesus still did not answer, and so Pilate was amazed.

Jesus or Barabbas

[6] At the festival Pilate used to release for the people a prisoner whom they requested. [7] There was one named Barabbas, who was in prison with rebels who had committed murder during the rebellion. [8] The crowd came up and began to ask Pilate to do for them as was his custom. [9] Pilate answered them, "Do you want me to release the King of the Jews for you?" [10] For he knew it was because of envy that the chief priests had handed him over. [11] But the chief priests stirred up the crowd so that he would release Barabbas to them instead. [12] Pilate asked them again, "Then what do you want me to do with the one you call the King of the Jews?"

[13] Again they shouted, "Crucify him!"

[14] Pilate said to them, "Why? What has he done wrong?"

But they shouted all the more, "Crucify him!"

[15] Wanting to satisfy the crowd, Pilate released Barabbas to them; and after having Jesus flogged, he handed him over to be crucified.

Mocked by the Military

[16] The soldiers led him away into the palace (that is, the governor's residence) and called the whole company together. [17] They dressed him in a purple robe, twisted together a crown of thorns, and put it on him. [18] And they began to salute him, "Hail, King of the Jews!" [19] They were hitting him on the head with a stick and spitting on him. Getting down on their knees, they were paying him homage. [20] After they had mocked him, they stripped him of the purple robe and put his clothes on him.

Crucified between Two Criminals

They led him out to crucify him. [21] They forced a man coming in from the country, who was passing by, to carry Jesus's cross. He was Simon of Cyrene, the father of Alexander and Rufus.

[22] They brought Jesus to the place called Golgotha (which means Place of the Skull). [23] They tried to give him wine mixed with myrrh, but he did not take it.

[24] Then they crucified him and divided his clothes, casting lots for them to decide what each would get. [25] Now it was nine in the morning when they crucified him. [26] The inscription of the charge written against him was: The King of the Jews. [27] They crucified two criminals with him, one on his right and one on his left.

[29] Those who passed by were yelling insults at him, shaking their heads, and saying, "Ha! The one who would destroy the temple and rebuild it in three days, [30] save yourself by coming down from the cross!" [31] In the same way, the chief priests with the scribes were mocking him among themselves and saying, "He saved others, but he cannot

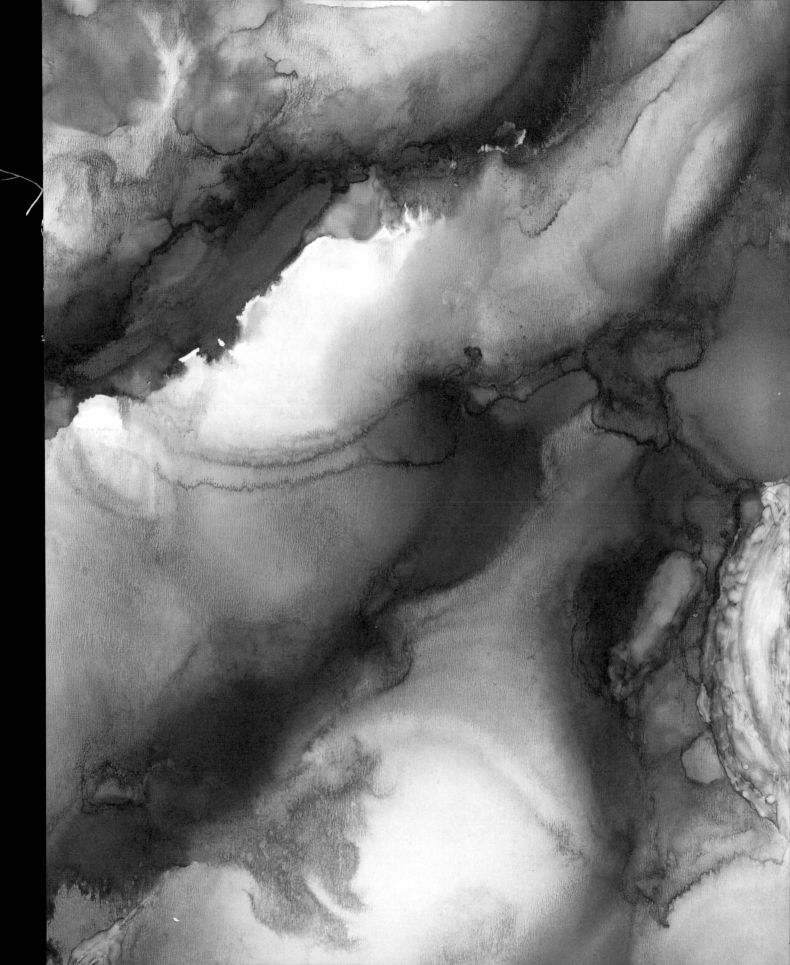

save himself! ³² Let the Messiah, the King of Israel, come down now from the cross, so that we may see and believe." Even those who were crucified with him taunted him.

The Death of Jesus

³³ When it was noon, darkness came over the whole land until three in the afternoon. ³⁴ And at three Jesus cried out with a loud voice, "Eloi, Eloi, lemá sabachtháni?" which is translated, "My God, my God, why have you abandoned me?"

³⁵ When some of those standing there heard this, they said, "See, he's calling for Elijah."

³⁶ Someone ran and filled a sponge with sour wine, fixed it on a stick, offered him a drink, and said, "Let's see if Elijah comes to take him down."

³⁷ Jesus let out a loud cry and breathed his last. ³⁸ Then the curtain of the temple was torn in two from top to bottom. ³⁹ When the centurion, who was standing opposite him, saw the way he breathed his last, he said,

"Truly this man was the Son of God!"

⁴⁰ There were also women watching from a distance. Among them were Mary Magdalene, Mary the mother of James the younger and of Joses, and Salome. ⁴¹ In Galilee these women followed him and took care of him. Many other women had come up with him to Jerusalem.

The Burial of Jesus

⁴² When it was already evening, because it was the day of preparation (that is, the day before the Sabbath), ⁴³ Joseph of Arimathea, a prominent member of the Sanhedrin who was himself looking forward to the kingdom of God, came and boldly went to Pilate and asked for Jesus's body. ⁴⁴ Pilate was surprised that he was already dead. Summoning the centurion, he asked him whether he had already died. ⁴⁵ When he found out from the centurion, he gave the corpse to Joseph. ⁴⁶ After he bought some linen cloth, Joseph took him down and wrapped him in the linen. Then he laid him in a tomb cut out of the rock and rolled a stone against the entrance to the tomb. ⁴⁷ Mary Magdalene and Mary the mother of Joses were watching where he was laid.

Isaiah 52:13-15

The Servant's Suffering and Exaltation

¹³ See, my servant will act wisely;
He will be raised and lifted up and greatly exalted.

¹⁴ Just as many were appalled at You—
His appearance was so disfigured
that he did not look like a man,
and his form did not resemble a human being—
¹⁵ so he will sprinkle many nations.
Kings will shut their mouths because of him,
For they will see what had not been told them,
and they will understand what they had not heard.

Isaiah 53:1-7

¹ Who has believed what we have heard?
And who has the arm of the LORD been revealed to?
² He grew up before him like a young plant
and like a root out of dry ground.
He didn't have an impressive form
or majesty that we should look at him,
no appearance that we should desire him.
³ He was despised and rejected by men,
a man of suffering who knew what sickness was.
He was like someone people turned away from;
he was despised, and we didn't value him.

⁴ Yet he himself bore our sicknesses,
and he carried our pains;
but we in turn regarded him stricken,
struck down by God, and afflicted.
⁵ But he was pierced because of our transgressions,
crushed because of our iniquities;
punishment for our peace was on him,
and we are healed by his wounds.
⁶ We all went astray like sheep;
we all have turned to our own way;
and the LORD has punished him
for the iniquity of us all.

⁷ He was oppressed and afflicted,
yet he did not open his mouth.
Like a lamb led to the slaughter
and like a sheep silent before her shearers,
he did not open his mouth.

Day 48
Holy Saturday

Luke 23:54-56

⁵⁴ It was the preparation day, and the Sabbath was about to begin. ⁵⁵ The women who had come with him from Galilee followed along and observed the tomb and how his body was placed. ⁵⁶ Then they returned and prepared spices and perfumes. And they rested on the Sabbath according to the commandment.

Matthew 27:62-66
The Closely Guarded Tomb

⁶² The next day, which followed the preparation day, the chief priests and the Pharisees gathered before Pilate ⁶³ and said, "Sir, we remember that while this deceiver was still alive he said, 'After three days I will rise again.' ⁶⁴ So give orders that the tomb be made secure until the third day. Otherwise, his disciples may come, steal him, and tell the people, 'He has been raised from the dead,' and the last deception will be worse than the first."

⁶⁵ "You have a guard of soldiers," Pilate told them. "Go and make it as secure as you know how." ⁶⁶ They went and secured the tomb by setting a seal on the stone and placing the guard.

Isaiah 53:8-12

⁸ He was taken away because of oppression and judgment;
and who considered his fate?
For he was cut off from the land of the living;
he was struck because of my people's rebellion.
⁹ He was assigned a grave with the wicked,
but he was with a rich man at his death,
because he had done no violence
and had not spoken deceitfully.

¹⁰ Yet the L<small>ORD</small> was pleased to crush him severely. When you make him a guilt offering, he will see his seed, he will prolong his days, and by his hand, the L<small>ORD</small>'s pleasure will be accomplished.

¹¹ After his anguish,
he will see light and be satisfied.
By his knowledge,
my righteous servant will justify many,
and he will carry their iniquities.
¹² Therefore I will give him the many as a portion,
and he will receive the mighty as spoil,
because he willingly submitted to death,
and was counted among the rebels;
yet he bore the sin of many
and interceded for the rebels.

They went and secured the tomb... MATTHEW 27:66

Day 49
Resurrection Sunday

Luke 24:1-49
Resurrection Morning

¹ On the first day of the week, very early in the morning, they came to the tomb, bringing the spices they had prepared. ² They found the stone rolled away from the tomb. ³ They went in but did not find the body of the Lord Jesus. ⁴ While they were perplexed about this, suddenly two men stood by them in dazzling clothes. ⁵ So the women were terrified and bowed down to the ground.

"Why are you looking for the living among the dead?"

asked the men. ⁶ "He is not here, but he has risen! Remember how he spoke to you when he was still in Galilee, ⁷ saying, 'It is necessary that the Son of Man be betrayed into the hands of sinful men, be crucified, and rise on the third day'?" ⁸ And they remembered his words.

⁹ Returning from the tomb, they reported all these things to the Eleven and to all the rest. ¹⁰ Mary Magdalene, Joanna, Mary the mother of James, and the other women with them were telling the apostles these things. ¹¹ But these words seemed like nonsense to them, and they did not believe the women. ¹² Peter, however, got up and ran to the tomb. When he stooped to look in, he saw only the linen cloths. So he went away, amazed at what had happened.

The Emmaus Disciples

¹³ Now that same day two of them were on their way to a village called Emmaus, which was about seven miles from Jerusalem. ¹⁴ Together they were discussing everything that had taken place. ¹⁵ And while they were discussing and arguing, Jesus himself came near and began to walk along with them. ¹⁶ But they were prevented from recognizing him. ¹⁷ Then he asked them, "What is this dispute that you're having with each other as you are walking?" And they stopped walking and looked discouraged.

CONTINUED

their joy, he asked them, "Do you have anything here to eat?" [42] So they gave him a piece of a broiled fish, [43] and he took it and ate in their presence.

[44] He told them, "These are my words that I spoke to you while I was still with you—that everything written about me in the Law of Moses, the Prophets, and the Psalms must be fulfilled." [45] Then he opened their minds to understand the Scriptures. [46] He also said to them, "This is what is written: The Messiah would suffer and rise from the dead the third day, [47] and repentance for forgiveness of sins would be proclaimed in his name to all the nations, beginning at Jerusalem. [48] You are witnesses of these things. [49] And look, I am sending you what my Father promised. As for you, stay in the city until you are empowered from on high."

Psalm 16:9-11

[9] Therefore my heart is glad
and my whole being rejoices;
my body also rests securely.
[10] For you will not abandon me to Sheol;
you will not allow your faithful one to see decay.
[11] You reveal the path of life to me;
in your presence is abundant joy;
at your right hand are eternal pleasures.

Hymn
Up from the Grave He Arose

Text and Tune: Robert Lowry, 1874

rose a vic - tor from the dark do - main, and He

lives for - e - ver, with His saints to reign. He a -

rose! He a - rose! Hal - le - lu - jah! Christ a - rose!
(He a- rose) (He a- rose)

Hallelujah! Christ arose!

SHE READS TRUTH *is a worldwide community of women who read God's Word together every day.*

Founded in 2012, She Reads Truth invites women of all ages to engage with Scripture through daily reading plans, online conversation led by a vibrant community of contributors, and offline resources created at the intersection of beauty, goodness, and Truth.

WHERE DID I STUDY?

O HOME
O OFFICE
O COFFEE SHOP
O CHURCH
O A FRIEND'S HOUSE
O OTHER

WHAT WAS I LISTENING TO?

ARTIST:

SONG:

PLAYLIST:

WHEN DID I STUDY?

MORNING

AFTERNOON

NIGHT

My closing prayer:

WHAT WAS HAPPENING IN MY LIFE?

WHAT WAS HAPPENING IN THE WORLD?

MONTH	DAY	YEAR

END DATE